Uncommon Sense

An Autistic Journey

Library and Archives Canada Cataloguing in Publication
Title: Uncommon sense : an autistic journey / by Adam Mardero.
Names: Mardero, Adam, author.
Identifiers: Canadiana (print) 20210225548 | Canadiana (ebook) 20210225572 | ISBN 9781988989358
  (softcover) | ISBN 9781988989396 (EPUB)
Subjects: LCSH: Mardero, Adam. | LCSH: Autistic people—Canada—Biography. | LCSH: Self-acceptance. |
  LCGFT: Autobiographies.
Classification: LCC RC553.A88 M37 2021 | DDC 616.85/8820092—dc23

Cover Art: Adam Mardero
Editor: Ella Jane Myers

Published by:
Latitude 46 Publishing
info@latitude46publishing.com
Latitude46publishing.com

We gratefully acknowledge the support of the Ontario Arts Council in the production of this book.

ONTARIO ARTS COUNCIL
CONSEIL DES ARTS DE L'ONTARIO
an Ontario government agency
un organisme du gouvernement de l'Ontario

Printed and bound in Canada on 100% recycled paper.

Uncommon Sense

An Autistic Journey

By Adam Mardero

In loving memory of Judy McKenty. Thank you for showing me that weirdness is something to be cherished, and for teaching me Autism is a gift beyond measure. You made our family just a little bit stranger ... and in the process, a lot more awesome. You will be dearly missed.

A Few Thoughts On Language ...

It bears mentioning here that Asperger's Syndrome is no longer considered an official diagnostic label by the fifth edition of the *Diagnostic and Statistical Manual of Mental Disorders (DSM)*. It has since been replaced by the term "Autism Spectrum Disorder" (ASD) to reflect autism's nature as a condition with many variations. This is a change I mostly agree with (though I, like many of my fellow advocates, really dislike the presence of the word 'disorder'), as it paves the way for a more inclusive understanding of what it means to be autistic. I was, however, diagnosed during the period in which Asperger's *was* considered one of many types of autism. As such, the Asperger's label has become important to my personal history. I do not use the term with any intention of being elitist or divisive, only out of recognition for the role the diagnosis has played in my life. Because of this, I have referred to both Asperger's and autism/ Autism Spectrum Disorder.

As well, the autistic community tends to prefer identity-first language ("I am autistic") rather than person-first ("I am a person with autism") because autism is very much viewed as a part of who we are and how our brains work. It cannot be separated from a person without drastically changing who they are. I am in complete agreement with my community on this, though in the interest of both accurately conveying the words used by others in dialogue and avoiding too much repetition, I have chosen to use both person-first and identity-first language throughout. I tend toward identity-first language for myself as well.

CHAPTER 1

1988 was a big year. It was when *Super Mario Bros. 3* came out in Japan, and when *Die Hard* landed in theatres (which I maintain is the best Christmas movie ever made). It was also the year of my birth, and unfortunately my parents divorced soon after. You see, my mom struggled with mental health issues as a result of childhood trauma. I'm not at liberty to get into details, but abuse was involved, and while she was able to get through much of life without being consciously aware of the toll it took on her psyche, eventually the cork popped. Her mental health declined, and my parents' marriage disintegrated. Because of this, they parted ways and I ended up living with my dad — an elementary school teacher — once the dust had settled.

Their separation was only the beginning of the story for me though. Not long afterward, my dad met a fellow teacher named Trish while working at St. Francis School in the special education department, and by 1992, she became my stepmother. The emergence of this new family dynamic wreaked havoc on my brain. It was a lot to process all at once, and our initial relationship was tense as a result. In retrospect, this difficulty with change was obviously due to the fact I am autistic. At the time though, we all lacked such vocabulary in our family lexicon. All I knew was I didn't like it. Not one bit.

To quote Peter Parker at the beginning of Sam Raimi's 2002

Spider-Man movie, "if someone told you this was a happy tale ... someone lied." My life was more complicated than it appeared, and it so often felt as though others couldn't comprehend the intense maelstrom of emotions going through my young brain — heck most of the time, neither could I. I just knew certain things made me extremely uncomfortable; food texture, smell, visual appearance, even doing homework. Each one of these became a potential flashpoint between us, as Trish and my dad tried to assert dominance and be stern in a situation they felt was best solved through discipline and order. That *was* the prevailing educational and parenting logic of the time after all, and my parents — being teachers themselves — were nothing if not up on the literature. The problem was, this didn't work on me and I dug in my heels, becoming even more intransigent in response. I was adrift, and in deeper waters than I was even aware. I didn't *want* to be argumentative or disruptive, but I had no other way to communicate the distress I felt.

The thing was, I did in fact love Trish a great deal. When we weren't butting heads, she was actually a lot of fun to be around. She had a good sense of humour, and genuinely seemed to care deeply for both my father and me. It was just that I found the situation extremely overwhelming and hated that she wanted to be my mother so soon after my actual mom and dad had split. I wasn't ready for that. But I also resented my mom for not being around more than every second weekend. In short, life was a mess.

From what Trish and my dad have described of those early years, my behaviour and outbursts kept them up often, and our entire family was on edge. According to my dad, everything about me was extreme: I was intensely fixated on things I found interesting to the point of obsession; I needed to completely, exhaustively finish one thing before I moved on to another; I preferred playing alone and had difficulty making friends; and, most notably to everyone around me in the family, I was extremely defiant when I didn't get my way. In addition to fights over dinner menu preferences born of sensory processing issues, screaming matches would frequently erupt over the smallest things. My zia (the Italian word for "aunt" in case you aren't familiar with the language) once wanted me to wait until after coffee to open gifts on my birthday, for example, and I was having none of it; I immediately created a scene, crying and shouting until they let me.

While I now see my past behaviour as a reaction to uncomfortable changes in my environment *combined* with undiagnosed autism, my dad and zia chalked it all up to messy but simple divorce-related emotions. Trish, however, suspected there might be something more to the story. She pushed for me to be seen by a professional with the school board, and both my dad and mom agreed, though not without reservations. I don't think either of them really thought it was possible that I was anything other than "normal" or *neurotypical* (meaning without what are commonly referred to as "neurodevelopmental disorders" or "mental health challenges"). From their perspectives, I was simply acting the way any kid going through a tough life change would. As my mom tells it, while she did notice I didn't like making eye contact, and it took me a while to become comfortable with hugging people (though I eventually came to love it), she never really thought there was anything drastically different about me compared to other kids. Between Trish's thoughts and my prior history of childhood epilepsy though, my mom and dad went along with her request to get me checked out. After all, better safe than sorry, right?

And so, with that decided, my dad picked me up at school one day (I was in third grade at the time) and told me we had to head to the board office for an appointment with someone he called a *psychometrist*. According to him, her name was Mrs. Perreira and she was just going to ask me some questions and get me to do school work while she watched. I groaned.

When we got there, Mrs. Perreira was standing in the lobby waiting for us. She told my dad he could wait there then led me down the hall and to one of the unused utility rooms where staff kept old resource documents and other educational materials.

It was dimly lit and had only a single window, out of which the parking lot could be seen.

"Hello Adam," she began. She had cropped red hair and a smile on her face. "I don't want you to be nervous. My name is Sue. It's nice to meet you."

Despite saying she didn't want me to be nervous, anxiety had already gripped my young brain. Everything about this day was strange and off: I wasn't at school; I wasn't with my friends … it felt like everything was falling apart.

"Hi Mrs. Perreira," I replied, not feeling comfortable using her first name. After all, that wasn't done … was it?

"So today, I just want to talk to you a bit about school and do some fun activities with you. I promise there's absolutely no pressure. How does that sound?"

It actually didn't sound so bad, so I smiled up at her. With my anxiety subsiding a bit, Mrs. Perreira didn't seem so scary anymore. I felt myself coming around to her.

"Good." Sue smiled back at me and motioned for me to make my way over to the table at the centre of the room. We sat on opposite ends facing each other, and once I was properly situated, Mrs. Perreira reached into her bag and produced some workbooks. Placing them on the table, she looked at me.

"Alright Adam, so let's start with this one here. I want you to look at the pictures on this side and find the missing part in the similar looking ones on the opposite side of the page. Do you think you can do that?"

I nodded eagerly. It was matching. I liked this kind of thing, and my enthusiasm showed. While I occasionally struggled to find the missing details, I was determined to succeed. I had to! Before long, I had completed the assignment, and I looked up at Sue.

"Well done. Now I have some more complex shape and colour patterns for you to work through. Want to try them?"

"Yes," I replied, grinning. It couldn't be this easy, could it? I was missing school for this?

I felt like the luckiest kid alive.

The shape testing continued for twenty minutes or so, though it felt like far less. Enjoying something will do that. Next were blocks, and despite some trial and error, I generally matched the patterns I was asked to reproduce easily enough. For a while, things felt fairly straightforward, and I began to fall into a sense of complacency with the testing. My concentration started to wander, and I began to get fidgety and restless. I didn't know why this was being done, but I knew I wasn't struggling very much with it.

I've got this! I remember thinking to myself. Which of course is what made the next part sting as much as it did. Sue pulled some green tennis balls out of her bag, and here my enthusiasm began to cool slightly. I've never been good at sports; I can't catch things or get my body to perform in such nuanced ways. My face immediately betrayed the dread I felt.

"It's okay Adam," Sue began. "I'm going to see how good you are at catching and remembering things next. I promise it won't be that bad."

"Okay," I said, slightly nervous but determined to keep going. She nodded and began the test. Sue would point to a spot on the table where she wanted me to place the ball then throw it to me, judging my ability to catch and remember where to place it. I found this difficult; there was too much going on at once! Too much sensory information to keep track of. I struggled to remember where Sue had pointed and found my brain unable to task-switch to catching, then back to memory in order to place the ball on the correct spot. I was rapidly becoming frustrated and overwhelmed. Anger rose in me and I scowled and wiped the tears from my eyes. But I refused to give up.

No. I won't let this test beat me!

With renewed determination, I did the best I could to complete the evaluation, and when we were done, Sue seemed genuinely taken aback by my level of persistence. The next portion of the testing was no better though and involved filling in designs on a sheet of paper with a strict time limit. I've never done well with time limits, and as I was faced with one then, I once again began to feel overwhelmed and unable to think clearly. It was too much pressure. How could anyone be expected to function that way?

I did the best I could, yet again refusing to give up even in the face of such a difficult challenge. I breathed a sigh of relief, however, when we moved to verbal reasoning and reading. These were things I could handle far more effectively, though the subject matter surprised me. The questions were about how I would handle hypothetical social situations with my peers and authority figures. There were several times I didn't quite understand what she was asking at first, but when she repeated herself more slowly and I had a chance to process, I was able to answer her well enough. She smiled from across the table once we had made our way through the question-and-answer section of the test.

"That was a great way to end off Adam. Good job."

"Thanks." I beamed proudly.

"I just have a few more questions for you if that's okay?" Sue pulled a line notepad out of her bag and clicked the button on her pen. I nodded, finding it slightly uncomfortable to hold her gaze for an extended period of time, but doing my best to not make it noticeable.

"Your parents tell me you're a bit argumentative at home," she began, and immediately my heart sank. *They'd told her about that? How could they?* "How does all of that make you feel?"

"I don't know," I replied, and I was being honest. There was such a maelstrom of emotions whirling in my mind and chest in those years I wasn't even consciously aware of any of them. "I don't know why I argue with my stepmom, okay? I just don't like being told what to do!"

"I understand that," Sue answered pensively, tapping her pen on the pad while she spoke. "Can you tell me why you think you might behave better at school than at home?"

"School is school, I guess. I don't know ..."

Sue smiled softly at me as she rose from her chair. She put her hand out for mine.

"We should probably get you back to your dad. Come on, I'll show you the way."

§

Sue was, of course, conducting a battery of standard intellectual assessment tests in addition to some emotional and behavioural evaluations. The results were then referred to Dr. Jackson, a local child psychiatrist, who met briefly with me a few times as well. My zia and nona did a lot for me as a kid — changing my diapers when I was super little and taking me to appointments at Sick Kids in Toronto for my epilepsy (with which I'd been diagnosed one terrifying day after having a massive seizure and being rushed to the hospital) — and they took me to these meetings, too. They often stood idly by as Dr. Jackson and I interacted. After a few weeks had passed, Trish, my dad, and my mom officially received a request for a consultation from Dr. Jackson's office. The details are somewhat foggy, with each of my parents having a slightly different account of the evening: my dad swears it was only he and Trish who attended, while my mom is adamant she was there too. In light of that, I've simply assumed over the years they were all present, especially since my mom vividly recalls several aspects of her interaction with Dr. Jackson that night.

Based on what I know of my parents' personalities, interpersonal dynamics, and lives during that time, I can only imagine how awkward they each must have felt as they met in the waiting room outside Dr. Jackson's office. In the years since, Trish has confirmed many of her earliest conversations with my mom felt strange, and that night would have been no different. Nevertheless, she and my mom have always respected each other and eventually even came to have a good rapport — a fact that no doubt made my father deeply uncomfortable. I can picture it now — my dad's face turning beet red as the two chatted about everything from home ownership to overbearing Italian families. The 1990s were a different era after all. While in the present day, befriending an ex and their current partner is virtually a non-issue unless things ended particularly badly, for them it wasn't so easy. The three of them were very much figuring it out as they went along.

When Dr. Jackson finally summoned them in, I'm sure everyone was relieved.

Little did they know the most challenging part was yet to come.

What happened next has become such an oft-repeated piece of lore between my mom and me that it almost feels as though I was actually there. She describes Dr. Jackson as a stiff, clinical man with an unpleasant demeanour — a depiction I've since learned to be quite accurate from friends who also saw him as kids. My dad often shares how the diagnosis process frightened him, and he recalls sitting nervously with me at the psychiatric hospital during an earlier visit with Dr. Jackson, waiting for me to go in and get mentally poked and prodded. It must have been awful, and while I don't remember any of it, my heart goes out to him all the same.

Anyway, on that night with all my parents, Dr. Jackson outlined the primary challenges he'd observed in me: poor emotional regulation and reciprocity, poor social cue recognition, and aggressive, argumentative behaviour. In his professional opinion, I had something called *Asperger's Syndrome*, which at the time was still considered a distinct form of autism. In fact, so scarring and terrifying were the final words of his report, they stuck in my parents' minds ever since: "I'm afraid young Adam will never be able to fall in love, form meaningful relationships with others, or indeed possibly even effectively communicate with them," my mother remembers him saying, "probably for life."

Though my mom is fond of telling me she never took his words seriously (and in fact, famously ... or infamously, if you were him maybe ... told him "You're wrong!" as she walked out of the office), my dad and Trish had a slightly longer journey ahead of them. After the initial diagnosis, they embarked on a quest to learn everything they could about Asperger's and what it meant for me. Fortunately, the more they absorbed, the more comfortable they became with the new normal they were adopting. After all, once you understand something, it becomes a known quantity you can work with, and the same was true for Trish and my dad during those years. It didn't quite end their worries about me — as my father tells it, they remained concerned about my future for years, and it would be some time before I worked through the big feelings I was experiencing. But that was the point at which my dad and Trish decided to make the best of the situation, and to simply let me be who I was supposed to be. In hindsight, their opting to *not* presume inability simply based on a diagnosis is what allowed me to come to believe in myself and ultimately led me to neurodiversity by practicing some of its principles before any of us even had the words for it. It's something I'm eternally grateful for.

CHAPTER 2

Let's rewind for a minute to 1994, only a few years prior to my diagnosis. We had just moved into a new house, in a new neighbourhood, on a street called Ursa Court. My parents have told me in the years since then, they wanted a bigger home in which to really start their family. Hence the move into what I thought of at the time as a mansion. There were four bathrooms total (including a separate one in my parents' bedroom), and it even had a purely decorative room we only used on special occasions. That room had a built-in shelf on the far wall that was always crammed with books, so I came to think of it as the library. Even back then, I loved libraries. This made sense; my dad used to read to me every night before bed, and it always felt good to lose myself in the story.

The move wasn't really the most pressing issue on my mind though. I was also grappling with the reality that my little sister Ella was about to be born, and other siblings were sure to follow soon after. So there I was, dealing with both turbulent feelings about my changing family situation, and with the uncertainty of fitting in on an unfamiliar street. Kids on the autism spectrum often don't handle changes of any kind all that well, and unfortunately for me, I was practically swimming in a sea of it, getting swallowed by the waves.

Looking back on the whole situation, I really empathize with Link from *The Legend of Zelda: Ocarina of Time*. He too was unique among the children of the forest because he didn't have a fairy companion of his own, and as such was often alone and unable to relate to the other kids in his village. This was exactly how I felt as I tried to navigate the social challenges on my new street. At first, I found myself hanging out with two brothers, Reggie and Dale, who lived in a brown brick house next to a rock pit where most of the neighbourhood kids played — both facts that I immediately took note of. On the day I met them, we spent an hour or so in their garage. Reggie owned a Sega Game Gear and a copy of *Sonic The Hedgehog* and I was entranced. It had full colour graphics and a back-lit screen; two things that were absolutely mind-blowing in 1994. It was really cool and I knew I had to try it.

We spent some time together that afternoon, with me annoying Reggie to no end in my attempts to learn about the Game Gear. Before long, the two brothers were summoned in for lunch by their dad, and I crossed the street back to my house. They told me they'd be back in a little while, and being the impatient kid I was, I figured I'd wait for them in my garage. After all, how long could they take?

What felt like an eternity passed (even though at most it had only been twenty minutes), and I was starting to feel restless. And bored. *Where could they have gone?* I found myself getting frustrated as I waited and kept checking the rock pit to see if I had missed their triumphant return. Eventually I spotted someone playing in the rocks. Wondering if my new playmates had come back, I made my way back across the street.

"Hi," I began, suddenly feeling awkward as I saw the boy playing in the rock pit was not, in fact, Reggie or Dale.

"Hi," he replied, glancing up at me then back down at the rock slab he had been drawing on with a smaller rock. I shifted in my place nervously.

"I'm sorry," I started. "I was playing with Reggie and Dale and I thought they were back. I didn't mean to bug you."

"It's okay," the boy answered. "I'm Mitch."

"My name's Adam," I replied. Mitch was a lanky boy, with

tousled, dirty blond hair hanging in a mop from his head. He had an infectiously warm smile and I started to feel at ease.

"Do you wanna play with me?" Mitch asked.

"Sure." I replied, climbing over several boulders, the starkly black and jagged kind Sudbury is infamous for, as I moved deeper in. "What are we playing?"

"School." Mitch beamed with pride as my heart sank.

"Really?" I sighed. Somehow, this wasn't what I'd had in mind.

§

After my fateful first meeting with Mitch in the Ursa Court rock pit, he and I became fast friends. Friendship hadn't always come easily to me. It wasn't so much that I didn't get along with other kids, but I found myself far more engrossed in my own obsessive passions. The other kids weren't usually able to keep up with me, and they also felt very strange. I often didn't really know how to approach them. I was always nice and friendly, but actually crossing that barrier into friend territory was something that didn't come as naturally. No matter what I did, it just always felt as though a glass wall separated us. There was this sense of detachment — as though I could never be one of them in any way. It went beyond normal introversion (though I was that too, which compounded things). It just felt so awkward to play with other kids, and it was far easier to just focus on my own little world. It was more comfortable in there anyway, safely removed from a social order I didn't fully understand.

My friendship with Mitch was different. Right from the beginning, we seemed to understand each other, and we quickly found ourselves doing everything together. I may not have been the most enthusiastic about playing school with him, for example, but we had lots of other common interests. We loved playing video games on the Super Nintendo. We also invented cartoon characters complete with detailed backstories and drew comic books. We even made our own paper cut-out toys based on our favourite TV shows and games we both enjoyed.

He seemed to get just as passionate as I did about our shared interests, and we each loved going down the rabbit hole and living in fantasy worlds of our own creation. With Mitch, I never worried about him finding me annoying when I got excited about the things I loved because usually he was right there with me doing the same thing.

Mitch and I were both unique and different from other kids in our own ways, and it went far beyond having the same passion for our shared interests. Neither of us were macho nor athletic, we tended to feel our emotions bubbling closer to the surface. We also both knew what it felt like to be 'weird' — that catch-all school yard term that looking back referred to all sorts of things; being gay, effeminate, neurodivergent, nerdy, or even just because you happened to wear the wrong graphic tee to school that day despite no one telling you which the correct one was beforehand. There was no shortage of reasons why kids called other kids 'weird', and Mitch and I fit a great many of them between us. I've found as an adult that the closest friendships I've made in my life have been with fellow neurodivergent people, whether either of us realized it at the time or not. Mitch has never been confirmed to be anything other than neurotypical, but it honestly wouldn't surprise me to learn he, too, was neurodivergent in his own way. Our people tend to seek each other out almost instinctively.

Neither of us yet knew precisely to what extent we didn't fit the social mold, we just enjoyed that, at last, we'd found someone who understood the other on a deeper level. Even so, befriending Mitch had unintended consequences; namely, it brought me into contact with the rest of the neighbourhood kids.

§

No childhood story is complete without a bully. An antagonist. That one kid who rules with an iron fist and forces a scrappy underdog to rise to the challenge and face them. Link had Mido — the arrogant ruler of his forest village — and in my case, her name was Kay. Kay was the leader of the Ursa Court gang. She had curly black hair and carried herself with an air of intimidation that would make any kid tremble. Basically, she was a living, breathing tough girl trope (think Helga Pataki from *Hey Arnold!*, Angelica Pickles from *Rugrats*). She was the dictator of the rock pit, and inspired fear in us all, Mitch included. Without realizing it, Mitch and I had committed the ultimate act of rebellion: we dared to be friends right under her nose. Mitch and Kay had always been close — she was one of his first friends on the street, and they'd known each other for several years by that point. I assumed Kay feared for her friendship with him and potential loss of control by bringing me into the mix, though I couldn't be sure. Her motivations were a complete mystery to me. Regardless of her reasons, she set to work terrorizing us all into line. Facing a bully is hard for any kid. For someone autistic, even if I didn't realize I was at the time, it was even harder.

Kay didn't start off by overtly bullying me — no, that would come later. Initially, she attempted to twist the situation to her advantage by acting like my friend and trying to turn Mitch and me against each other. There's one specific example that comes to mind. One day, Kay spotted me on the street heading toward the rock pit from my house and called out to me.

"Hey Adam, over here!"

A cold sweat covered me as soon as I heard her. Even though I hadn't yet come to understand the full extent of her ruthlessness, I was already intimidated by her. Nevertheless, I made my way over.

"... Hi ... Kay."

"Oh, don't look so scared, Adam." Kay sneered. "Can't a girl say hi to the new kid on the street?"

"Well, yeah ... sure you can," I replied, somewhat unsure of what to make of the situation. She was being nice ... so maybe she wasn't really as scary as I'd thought?

"Good! So, I see you and Mitch have gotten to be pretty good friends, eh?"

"We have!" I answered her, smiling happily. Kay grinned, placing her hands on her hips.

"Well, I have a little prank I want to play on him, and I think he'll think it's hilarious. As his new friend, I thought you might want to be in on it."

This is the part where I should have seen red flags and run fast in the opposite direction. It's the kind of situation which, in adulthood, and with thirty-odd years of experience navigating life with an autistic brain under my belt, I would now know to steer clear of. Unfortunately, as a kid I tended to be far more oblivious.

"Sure," I replied at last, not completely sold, but swept up in the excitement of the moment.

"Awesome. So here's what I want you to do. I want you to go into Mitch's area in the rocks ... you know ... where he plays school. And once you're there, I want you to smash it up a bit. We're going to trick him into thinking it was the wind or some other random thing that did it. Sounds funny, doesn't it?"

In truth, it didn't ... not at all. Maybe it was funny to kids who weren't weird (or in hindsight, neurodivergent). Maybe Kay was trying to help me. I wasn't sure either way, but she seemed to be accepting me, and that was a powerful drug. Up until that point, I could count on only a few fingers the people I felt truly accepted me. Being offered acceptance, even if it was by Kay, sent my mind spinning. Any misgivings I might have felt at the time were mitigated by this. I nodded and set to work causing disarray in Mitch's carefully organized play area while Kay stood back and watched, thrilled with herself as her scheme took form. Once I was done, I walked back over to Kay just in time; Mitch was headed back toward us, and the prank was about to begin. At that point, Kay told me she needed to go eat dinner, leaving me alone. Naturally, it didn't take long for Mitch to notice what had happened and he came stomping back over to me

"What happened to my class?"

"Um," I began, tripping over my words. "Well ... you see

Mitch ... the ... ah ... wind did it."

Mitch stood there looking at me skeptically, his eyebrow cocked as he sized up my admittedly terrible explanation.

"... The wind did it? Really Adam?"

"Yeah. I ... saw it myself ..."

"But there were lots of heavy things the wind couldn't have blown over," Mitch retorted in anger. "Are you telling me they just happened to fall over too?"

"Um ... yes?"

It was at that point, as I processed how visibly upset Mitch was, that I started to realize what Kay had done. She hadn't been trying to pull a prank on Mitch — if she'd really been doing that, she would have stuck around to see the look on his face, told him it was a joke, and helped him clean up. No, she'd done something far worse: she'd set us up to be at each other's throats. And I had played right into her hands.

"Wait, no. I'm sorry. It was Kay — she told me to do it."

Mitch deflated somewhat. I heaved a sigh of relief.

"Why would she do that?" he asked. "And why would you go along with it?"

"She scares me, okay?" I said, tearing up a bit. "And she was being nice to me, so I thought she'd accepted me. But I don't think she has."

"Definitely not," Mitch replied, face palming in frustration. "Don't you see what happened here? She tried to get us to fight. She wanted to break us up from being friends because she's jealous."

"You're right," I admitted. "But what can we do?"

"I have a pretty good idea." I inhaled sharply, anxiety rising.

Oh no, I thought. *Mitch isn't going to forgive me for this one, is he? I mean, Kay may have come up with the idea, but I was the one who did it. I betrayed him and I deserve it.*

"Want to go back to your house and play Donkey Kong Country?"

I couldn't help but smile. *Donkey Kong Country 2: Diddy's Kong Quest* for Super Nintendo was — and still is — one of our favourites. For Mitch to suggest it meant things were good between us. The anxiety emptied from my chest like hot air rushing out of a balloon.

"Do I ever." I replied. He smiled back.

"Good. But promise me two things: we don't let Kay stop us from being friends ever again."

"Deal." I confirmed. "What's the second thing?"

"*Never* do something like that again!"

It was an easy promise. The whole ordeal really flummoxed me though. How were some people so good at manipulating others like that? Kay was my age — 6 years old—and yet she'd somehow figured out how to understand her peers in a way I could only dream of. Moreover, she'd figured out how to get them to do what she wanted. Granted, it was through fear and intimidation, but even in such a crude form, it was a dark gift she seemed to have. I, on the other hand, was hopelessly socially awkward. I talked too much, I tended to overshare, and had no clue how to form lasting connections with most other kids. I knew I needed to learn more, and to figure out how to be more perceptive of others' tricks.

Mitch was actually invaluable for this. He's always had an uncanny ability to detect bullshit from a mile away. In fact, during one sleepover we had at her house, my mom shared with me afterwards how she felt he was observing and noting everything that went on. In this way, I like to think that we balanced each other out. I pulled him up into the sky with my drifting, floating, dreaming consciousness that saw the whole forest, while he pulled me back down to the ground when an individual tree needed our attention. I've learned more from Mitch about how to understand people than I've ever expressed to him, and I'm eternally grateful that Kay's scheme that day didn't end our nascent friendship in its tracks.

Kay remained a presence on the street and in both our lives, but after that, she was never again able to come between Mitch and me. In a strange way, it was one of many incidents that strengthened our bond and made it unbreakable. While the years would offer their own challenges, from that point on I knew Mitch was my ally and best friend.

§

Having realized her plot failed, Kay gave up trying to be nice and went for more overt bullying tactics from then on. After one particularly mean-spirited encounter with her later in 1999 during which she had called me fat, I ran home with tears in my eyes, desperate for any help from my parents. I've never been a "thin" person, but hearing those words hurt me badly. *Surely they'll help me*, I thought, heart pounding as I rushed in through the garage and slammed the laundry room door shut behind me. I didn't know how to deal with bullies at the time, and as much as I had the guts to get into screaming matches with Trish, the same could not always be said for my peers. I always felt so awkward, so uncomfortable in my own skin; it was like being covered in snakes and not knowing how to get them off.

Unfortunately, I would find no sympathy at home.

"Well if she's bullying you Adam, you need to get right out there and fight back."

Trish stood as she passed her advice along. She smiled sympathetically but her stance was resolute.

"But ... but ..."

"Adam, you can't let her get away with this," Trish continued. "If you don't stand up to her, she's just going to keep on doing this."

"I'm scared though."

"I know," she replied, "but I have an idea of what you can say back to her if she calls you fat again."

Leaning over to whisper in my ear, I smiled through my rapidly drying tears as I took in what Trish wanted me to say back to Kay. As scared as I was, I was newly galvanized.

Yup, I thought, *she won't know what hit her.*

I hugged Trish and ran back outside. In the words of William Shakespeare; once more unto the breach ...

§

"I bet you think you're so tough, standing there, don't you?"
We were deadlocked, as we had been for what seemed like
hours. I was quaking in my boots. Still I didn't let the fear rule
me — no small feat for a boy my age at the time.
"You just need to shut up, you hear me?" I screamed
at the top of my lungs, determined for all the kids in the
neighbourhood to hear. Certainly, the ones who were present
did. There came a point in the whole ordeal where, heart
pounding and nerves on edge, I stopped being afraid. Instead,
my sense of stubbornness took over and I dug my heels in. Kay
smirked, clearly finding this amusing, which made her cruel.
"You're pathetic, you know that?" she chuckled darkly as she
paced on the spot, sizing me up. I didn't dare move, and neither
did the other kids.
"None of them like you," she continued. "Not even Mitch.
They all told me so!"
"You're lying," I shot back, anger welling up ... and slight
fear. I knew intellectually she was wrong but ... what if she
wasn't?
No, I thought to myself, *don't give in to her. She's lying.* I
looked to all the other kids standing around, each of whom
bowed their heads, clearly not wanting to get involved. I was
hurt that Kay had them so wrapped around her finger, not one
came to my defence.
"I'm not pathetic," I shot back at last. "You're a bully. And
I'm Mitch's friend, and there's nothing you can do about it."
Frankly, the audacity of my younger self amazes me to
this day, and I think he had the same effect on young Kay. She
groaned as she threw her hands in the air in frustration.
"Fine you know what?" she began, her words like acid as
they emerged from her mouth. "You're a big, fat, loser."
With that, the moment I had been waiting for had come.
I was prepared. I had the perfect comeback. I looked at Kay,
surging with defiant pride, and declared:

"Well I might be fat, but you're stupid, and I can always lose weight!"

With that, all of the neighbourhood kids stopped and stared, suddenly captivated by what was going on. Kay appeared flummoxed. At that moment, had I been thinking tactically, I could have said any number of badass things and let the mic drop as I walked into the sunset victoriously.

Unfortunately, as is the curse with being a spectrum dweller, I wasn't that socially aware at the time.

"And my stepmom told me to say that."

The street went silent. Before I knew it, they started laughing hysterically. I didn't realize it at the time, but I had killed my own defence. And so, the saga of Kay the Bully went on. But on that day, I fought like a warrior. A true, awkward, socially anxious warrior.

CHAPTER 3

My dad and Trish are wonderful, kind-hearted and loving people who have each had long and storied education careers. My dad still gets stopped by former students and praised to this day for connecting with them when no other teacher could, while Trish won a lifetime achievement award after retiring from her role as the principal of one of Sudbury's biggest high schools. It's not hard to see why they were drawn to each other; they cared about the kids and teens in their charge, and always sought to bring out the best in them. This eventually extended to their own kids too, and there have been so many instances throughout our lives when my sisters, brother, and I have been lucky to have them in our corners. Especially Trish. She could be a downright force of nature when she wanted to be, and nothing could stand between her and what she knew needed to be done.

Unfortunately, this very same force of will brought us into conflict with each other more often than either of us would have liked. You see, in many ways, she and I are a lot alike; we're both extremely determined, stubborn, hard-headed people who care deeply and want to help others. The problem back then was, we were often on opposite sides of the same issues.

After I got diagnosed with Asperger's, Trish and my dad embarked on a quest to learn all they could about this mysterious new condition they'd been confronted with. I'm told they read copious amounts of books, talked to experts at the school board, and just generally sought to understand. Ultimately, they seem to have settled on a two-pronged approach; don't infantilize or presume incompetence, and also, be strict and enforce a rigid structure. Because autistic kids need structure and discipline, so said the prevailing wisdom of the time.

I've already explained a little about why parts of this approach didn't work for me, but I'd like to go a little more in depth with that here. The thing is, the first prong was absolutely critical; in a world where autistic and otherwise neurodivergent people are often shamed, infantilized, and made to feel less than, deciding to treat your autistic kid like a full human is a radical act of love. This was doubly true in the 1990s, when public understanding of neurodiversity and mental health was still in its infancy. That all three of my parents chose to do this in those days was extraordinary.

There is a potential dark side to this approach though, and it both ties in with the second prong, and is a pitfall Trish and my dad fell hard into. When you opt to not infantilize or presume incompetence, it's very difficult to walk the line between that and either assuming your child's diagnosis can be overcome, or simply ignoring it altogether. Given the rigidity and stern discipline Trish and my dad seemed to favour with me, it's pretty clear they fell into the former camp. They can be forgiven for thinking so too; it was the 90s, and we couldn't know what we didn't know. Even still, the combination of assuming Asperger's was something to be defeated, and not talking about it in anything but hushed or negative tones did little to make me want to understand how it related to my struggles. In fact, the opposite often became true. Asperger's started to feel like a dirty word, and my struggles came to feel like personal failures, rather than a result of my neurotype. Things like sensory issues around food and difficulties following the strict rules Trish and my dad had imposed were thought of as my being 'difficult' or 'argumentative' and I was therefore punished for them.

I know they were trying their best to navigate uncharted territory, but in fairness? So was I.

For this reason, I usually looked forward to visiting my mom every second weekend with every fibre of my being. When my parents divorced, she became an inpatient at our local psychiatric hospital for a time before getting her own apartment and tenuously beginning to rebuild her life. She knew she wanted to be involved, but by necessity it started off slowly at first — supervised afternoon visits and trips to McDonald's for dinner together. Once she'd found her footing as a parent, she bought a house and we settled into an arrangement where I spent every second weekend at her place. Going there felt like a refuge from the challenging environment that was living with my dad and step-mom and my excitement for these weekends was almost overwhelming. It was one of the few places I felt I could truly be myself without having to mask and conform to what felt like arbitrarily defined standards of 'appropriate' behaviour. Naturally, such masking, mixed with the tension between my parents and I, didn't bode well for my mental health as a kid. It was utterly exhausting. Because of this, I often felt like I was exploding with energy at the mere thought of escaping to my mom's house for a few days at a time.

On one specific weekend six months after my session with Sue, I was feeling more excited than usual to seek shelter with my mom. Ever since the diagnosis happened, I began to notice the word Asperger's used more and more at home, often accompanied by the aforementioned stricter rules and clashes over the most minute of things. Homework, for example, had to be done the *moment* I got home, and I wasn't allowed to do anything else until it was. Dinnertime? I had to eat exactly what was served and couldn't complain or voice my thoughts or else I'd be punished. I know that to many neurotypical people, these may seem like reasonable requirements, but neurodivergent people like myself often struggle with things like focus, energy levels, and sensory sensitivities. I needed transition time after school to detox from the day and get myself into home mode before I could even think of starting my homework. Likewise, certain foods just immediately set off my brain's *nope* response. I didn't even have to taste it; often, the sight was enough to cause immediate aversion. Of course, as a kid I lacked the ability to articulate any of this — I just knew it caused me intense internal anguish to even try. When combined with the already tense relationship I had with Trish because of her attempts to be my parent (because don't you know? I already have a mom), the emotional turmoil inside my brain threatened to become overwhelming. That particular week, it was almost too much to take.

A storm was brewing internally, and it consumed my thoughts, even though I tried not to let it. After all, mom and I were going treasure hunting at second-hand stores — which was one of our shared favourite things. We had planned an excursion to a place called The Barn Sale on the outskirts of town that my mom had spotted in a newspaper ad. It promised lots of vintage treasures to those who made the trek ... and so trek we would. I didn't want the emotional turmoil I felt to ruin the experience.

"Hi sweetie," My mom greeted me at the door as my dad dropped me off. She wore a baggy sweater with multi-coloured geometric shapes, and her hair was a recently-dyed vibrant shade of red. She smiled as I ran to her arms and hugged her. I was always very excited to see her, but that week had been particularly challenging. This fact betrayed itself as I embraced my mom with all my strength.

"It's good to see you, too." She chuckled as she hugged me back with one arm, using her free one to wave down at my dad standing in the driveway.

"Make sure to get him back in one piece," he shouted up at her.

"I always do, Herc," she replied. My mom closed the door as I made my way inside. In the background, I heard the muffled sound of my dad getting into his car, starting the engine, and driving off.

I was free. I should have been happy. After a week filled with emotionally exhausting battles over every little thing, I could breathe easily for the first time in days ... and yet this realization simply served to make me feel even more lost.

My mom noticed the pensive look on my face as we entered the kitchen. I immediately made for the fridge, where I grabbed the bottle of apple juice, poured myself a glass, and sat down at the kitchen table. Following behind me, she made sure the window was open wide and the air current generated by the ceiling fan wasn't blowing my way, then lit a cigarette and sat across from me. She reached for my hand in concern.

"Are you okay, Adam?"

"Yeah," I replied, taking a swig of juice from my glass. The amber liquid was sweet and pleasing as it hit my taste buds.

"Are you sure? You know you can always talk to me about anything."

"I know Mom." I forced a smile and looked at her across the table. "I just ... sometimes feel really sad and angry."

With that, the look on my mom's face shifted. Her eyes widened and her mouth drooped into a frown.

"Sad and angry?"

"Yeah. Sometimes I just want to disappear. Like it would be easier if I wasn't here."

"Oh Adam," my mom replied. She looked worried but struggled to maintain her composure. "You are so loved and valued. Both your dad and I, your sisters, and even Trish — we all love you so much. Don't keep this kind of thing in — it's not healthy. Believe me, I know ..."

My mom bowed her head and took another drag of her cigarette. "Something I learned when I was in hospital sweetie—emotions need to come out eventually. In my case, they did it pretty explosively and tore apart my life around the time you were born. They will find a way to bubble to the surface, no matter what you do. If they can't do it one way, they'll figure out another."

She was right of course, but all I could manage was a nod

and a half smile.

"I don't know how much you know about when Trish, your dad, and me met Dr. Jackson a few months ago ..." Mom began again, her tone mixing inquiry and explanation.

"Not much," I answered. *It was true—no one had told me anything.* "All I know is, one day, everyone started talking more about something called *Ass-burgers?* Mom, I don't want ass burgers!"

My mom laughed loudly. "No no sweetie. Not ass-burgers. *Asperger's.* It's a German word, I think."

"It's something Dr. Jackson said you had. He told us you'd struggle with being able to make friends and get close to people," she continued, "but I've never once believed it. This is proof; you feel your feelings deeply and truly, and you always have. And just look at Mitch; when you let someone into your world, it's all or nothing. So if you're feeling these big feelings, don't worry about pouring them all out on me. I can take it, and you need it."

I was silent for a moment as I processed mom's words. It shocked me that someone had said such things about me. It even enraged me a little. More than anything though, I laughed. After all it *did* sound ridiculous in light of the life I knew I was living. There was no way any of it could be true ... could it?

"You're right mom," I agreed at last and smiled. She reached her hand across the table and took mine.

"You're a smart, kind, loving, and wonderful boy. I'm so lucky to call you my son. Don't listen to what anyone says — not Dr. Jackson, not the other kids, not even Trish, your dad, or me. You can do whatever you set your mind to in this life."

There was no denying it; I felt lighter than I had all evening. The negative emotions drained out of me a little with my mother's words of encouragement and support. Almost as if to echo the sentiment, the sun shone more brightly through the window, and I felt its warm glow both on my skin and in my heart.

Obi-Mom Kenobi had spoken, and she was wise indeed.

CHAPTER 4

My mom is a very private person when it comes to her mental health, so I can't get into detail here about exactly what kinds of battles she's faced. Suffice it to say that terms like 'childhood trauma' and 'PTSD' have always been well known to her. When I was growing up, she simply referred to it as 'being sick' when she talked to me, but I've since come to learn just how strong and courageous she had to be through her own life struggles. She spent some time institutionalized, and even more time after that navigating the mental health system as an outpatient. Because of this, she was able to gain an almost Zen-like wisdom about emotions, self-regulation, and mental health in general ... at least that's what it felt like when she counselled me about it. It was hard-won wisdom of course, but it often helped her realize what was going on in my head, even when I didn't. She worked hard to listen to and validate my opinions and perspectives — which was why my words worried her as much as they did.

I now know that once I was out of earshot, my mom immediately called my dad and let him and Trish know what I'd said. While my dad was a bit skeptical at first, all three of them agreed that even after my diagnosis, they were still no closer to fully getting to the bottom of my emotional troubles. After some discussion, they agreed to seek out a therapist for me ... both to help with my emotional issues (because processing "big feels" is something those of us on the spectrum often struggle with) and hopefully to get a second opinion on Dr. Jackson's Asperger's diagnosis.

That was how we ended up going to see Dr. Miller, a kindly older psychiatrist who ran a practice out of her home in the suburbs of Sudbury. I didn't realize until years later how much Dr. Miller truly helped me out of a dark place in my life. When I had my first session with her, I remember her asking questions about things while I drew pictures of superheroes and spaceships. My interests haven't really changed.

"So, your parents tell me you like superheroes," she began as she watched me draw. I nodded and kept at it, intent on what I was creating. My eyes occasionally lifted from the paper in front of me and wandered the room as we spoke though, picking up on the details that surrounded me. I noticed that Dr. Miller's office was stark and lit with the pure white light of fluorescent bulbs. The table where we sat was off to one side, with a counter and sink behind me, and a large open closet behind her. There were toys neatly organized in bins at the mouth of the closet: a few old Transformers, a fighter jet, and some LEGO-like blocks of varying shapes and sizes. A musty smell like used books hung in the air. Dr. Miller jotted notes the whole time.

"I think they're cool," I dismissed. Remembering something, my eyes shot up to hers, suddenly full of energy. "I made up my own with my best friend ... want to see?"

"Certainly," she replied. Pointing to a funny-looking, lizard-like character I had drawn, she smiled and tapped it with her pen.

"Now who is that creature?"

"His name is Jaw Cracker," I explained. "He's a bad guy. Flibo needs to stop him."

"I see, I see," Dr. Miller responded thoughtfully, scratching her head in confusion. "And what's a fly-bo?"

"Not fly-bo," I laughed, flipping to the right page of my sketches and lifting it up to show her. "Flibo. He's half rat, half fly, and he's a detective. He lives in the sewers in a city called Ratville and tries to stop Jaw Cracker and his gang of criminals from committing crimes."

"My that's very imaginative Adam," commented Dr. Miller at last, appearing genuinely impressed. "You're quite creative, aren't you?"

"I like drawing and inventing stuff is all. I see cool things and I want to invent my own. My friend Mitch and I do this kind of thing all the time. Flibo is both of ours. Want to know about some of the superheroes we made up?"

Dr. Miller nodded. I don't think she really knew what she was getting herself into. After all, in typical neurodivergent fashion, when I got passionate about something I could talk — *a lot*. I proceeded to tell her for the next twenty minutes about Grasshopper Man and his sidekick Ant Man (I was dismayed when I found out Marvel had beat me to it with their own), and their gallery of villains. If Dr. Miller was ever annoyed, she didn't betray any sign of it and just let me talk. She allowed me to express myself in a way I often didn't feel allowed to by Trish and my dad, and she seemed to genuinely value what I said. My mom was the only other person who showed that much interest in my ideas and thought processes without trying to change me. In retrospect, it explained a lot about why I always behaved better for her than I did for my dad and Trish.

"It's a pleasure to talk to you Adam," Dr. Miller said once I'd finally given her an opening. "Tell me though, do you ever feel as though you just need to get your thoughts out like this before you lose your train of thought?"

"Well, yeah actually."

She nodded. "Your mom told me that you said you felt sad and angry inside. Why do you think that is?"

"I don't know," I began. "I guess I just don't like when my stepmom bosses me around and doesn't listen to me."

"I can understand that," Dr. Miller empathized. "It's hard to process these kinds of big feelings when we don't feel listened to, isn't it?"

I bobbed my head in agreement.

"Well Adam, I think I may have an idea how to help you. I'd

like you to come back and see me for a bit, and I'm also going to talk to your parents about some other things we can try. Would you like that?"

"Yes," I acquiesced, not knowing what else to say. After all, what *could* I say?

"Great. I'll talk to your parents and get everything set up." Dr. Miller got up to leave the room, but winked at me on her way out the door. "And next time, I want to hear more about your creations."

§

Dr. Miller ultimately ended up recommending to my parents that I take Ritalin. In her opinion, it would help me regulate my big feelings and focus more. From her perspective, I was going through a depressive episode related to both my complex feelings about the divorce, and to my neurodivergent brain wiring. Dr. Miller, however, disagreed with Dr. Jackson about exactly which form this wiring took. To her mind, it wasn't Asperger's as he had claimed—it was what was then known as Attention Deficit Disorder or ADD (which is now referred to as the inattentive subtype of ADHD instead). Regardless of who was right though, my parents agreed with her suggestion and I started a course of Ritalin not long after.

It's difficult to say exactly how long I took this medication for, but I will say that my memories of how it made me feel are spotty at best. On the one hand, I don't remember it making me feel any different at all, though this is almost certainly due to my lack of ability to understand my own experience of consciousness as a child. On the other hand, I do distinctly remember a moment at the end of one weekend visit with my mom when, after staring into a mirror by her entrance for a few moments, it suddenly dawned on me that I wanted to try to be less argumentative and at least attempt to make things work with Trish. Whether I realized it or not, the Ritalin had begun helping my brain process the internal emotional storm. It once more felt like I was Link, fighting my way through the dark of night on Hyrule Field as wave after wave of Stalfos (undead skeleton monsters) assaulted my position. Except this time, the dawn was coming, and as soon as it did, the monsters would recede back into the depths of the earth.

Despite how helpful it seemed to be, my dad didn't like how Ritalin made me behave. When we were talking about it years later while moving me into a new apartment in May of 2017, he looked at me and shook his head, telling me that it made me "act like a zombie." For that reason, I suspect the experiment only lasted a few months before I came off it.

Even still. It was enough. It had done its part to help me figure myself out a bit, and I'm grateful we gave it a shot all the same.

Ultimately, my parents also chose not to pursue a change of diagnosis from Asperger's to ADD either. Going back to what I said earlier about walking the line between not presuming incompetence, and assuming someone can overcome a diagnosis, after the Ritalin had helped a tad, my parents decided I was probably 'fine.' Superficially, I seemed to be after all; I was getting good marks at school, making friends, and had at least started trying to play nice with Trish, so they saw no reason to further the process.

What they didn't understand back then though was that both autism and ADHD explained different facets of why I was the way I was. My social struggles, naiveté, and hyperfixation were almost certainly due to being autistic, while my difficulty doing things like focusing on homework and regulating emotions were classic ADHD traits. Sometimes, the line between them even blurred so as to make it impossible to determine which was at play (or if, indeed, they were running my brain in two-player mode). As such, I've since sought out and received confirmation that both Dr. Jackson *and* Dr Miller were in fact correct; I am both autistic, and I have ADHD—a co-diagnosis that is now possible under the DSM-V. This felt extremely vindicating and validating.

CHAPTER 5

For all the diagnostic struggles and emotional challenges I faced as an autistic kid, my childhood growing up in the nineties was actually a fairly stereotypical one. This included going to a small local elementary school close to home. Around the same time that I'd been diagnosed with Asperger's, Trish had also been promoted to principal of St. Theresa School. It was quickly decided that I should follow her there for convenience's sake. I had no strong feelings about this plan either way — all I knew was I would be starting at a new school at the beginning of the new school year, and that made me both nervous and excited. It wasn't as though I was leaving Mitch *per se* — our friendship had forever been based on Ursa Court because he always went to a different school than I did — but even still, the anxiety of venturing forth from the safety of my home base into a whole new world was one I knew intimately well.

My first day at St. Theresa followed just about every first day cliché there is: I was ushered to the Grade 3 French Immersion classroom, where I was greeted by the most intimidating person I'd met up until that point in my life. She stood five foot four, with a pair of librarian spectacles resting on the bridge of her nose. She also had a look so stern it could make King Leonidas of ancient Sparta turn tail and run. She cracked a small, brittle smile as she welcomed me and asked me to take a seat. I obeyed without question and felt the gazes of all of my peers on me instantly as I made my way into the classroom proper. It was as though dozens of laser beams were being shot in my direction from each of their eyes, and it was all I could do to dive for the closest free desk.

"Class, my name is Madame Myer, and I'm your Grade 3 teacher. During this year, I will push you, I will challenge you, and I will not take any horsing around, is that clear?"

The entire class nodded. Satisfied she had made her point, Madame Myer turned back to the blackboard to begin the day's lesson, at which point I got excited. School had always thrilled me, and I was always precocious, no matter how much I typically pretended I didn't enjoy it.

"Good. Now open your notebooks. Today, we're going to start learning the basics of conjugating verbs ... in French."

We all heaved a collective sigh.

§

Getting used to a scary new teacher wasn't the only intimidating thing about starting at a new school; there was also the whole social angle ... something I hope by now I've established just how much I sucked at. Whether you attribute it to autism or not, there is no denying that I was an awkward and shy kid. Mitch and I always got along great, but it was more difficult than it had to be at school. At my old school, for example, I was always finding myself picked last during games. And, even though I had made one close friend, he ended up getting moved to a new school part way through the year, and no one told me. It was only after several days of hoping to find him at recess and not seeing him anywhere I realized the truth. I was lucky things changed at St. Theresa. It all began in Madame Myer's class as we slogged along through the millionth conjugation of the French verb *etre*.

"I'm so bored ...," I muttered under my breath, more to myself than anything as I doodled in the margins of my notebook. Admittedly, I should have been paying attention, but my mind wandered easily (something about that ADHD thing

Dr. Miller thought I had).

"You know, it's really not that bad when you stop paying attention," a quiet voice came from the desk next to me.

Looking over, I was surprised to see my neighbour trying to catch my attention. She was a slender girl, with shoulder length brown hair and bangs that covered most of her forehead. Resting on the bridge of her nose were a pair of glasses with thick, black plastic rims. She looked like a nerd and I instantly liked her.

"I'm Saria," she smiled.

"Adam," I replied shyly.

"I know," she answered, chuckling a little. "We were told we were getting a new kid before you walked in."

"Oh," I said, not sure how to respond. Saria grinned and kept talking, careful not to draw the attention of Madame Myer.

"It's cool, you seem normal enough."

"Yeah ... I suppose ..."

"Hey, do you want to play with us at recess?"

I was shocked. I was being asked to play at recess? Such a little thing, but for a kid like me, it was huge. In the vicious world of elementary school, your recess gang was your family. Your people. The very definition of social outcast in the schoolyard context was to be without friends to play with at recess. The fact that I was being asked to be part of that ... it was amazing.

"Sure," I replied. Saria smiled and nodded happily. I was filled with excitement. Unfortunately, I wasn't the only one who had taken notice of my changing social status.

"Mister Mardero." Madame Myer called, scowling. She raised her voice as she spoke, and I shrank five sizes in my seat. "I don't see how what you and Miss Mailloux are talking about could possibly be more important than this lesson, do you?"

Yes, I do, I thought, wanting so desperately to say the words. Instead, my response was wisely more measured.

"No Madame Myer."

"Well then," she replied, grinning darkly. "Perhaps you'd like to lead us in the conjugation of the verb *etre* into present tense?"

I sighed. I had been busted. Caught red-handed not paying attention in class. As I got to my feet, I steeled myself and began conjugating, desperate for the moment to be over and for the impending recess to begin. At least I had that to look forward to.

"Je suis, tu es, il est ..."

§

"Go. Get to the bridge. You need to take back the ship from the Empire."

Captain Pressot lay struggling against his wounds as he looked up at me. He clutched his chest in pain, blood staining his uniform.

"But sir, I —"

"Don't argue with me AM-75," he replied, "Go!"

Nodding solemnly, I made my way down the corridor to the ship's control room, intent on fulfilling my mission. My left hand folded out of the way to reveal the built-in missile launcher embedded in my forearm, and my optical sensors shifted to tactical mode. I saw movement ahead, on the other side of the bridge door, and readied myself for the battle that was to come. Arriving at the hatch, I used my connection to the ship's computer to override the lock. There were some advantages to be had in being a cyborg.

What I saw next sent shivers down my robotic spine. Standing there, crimson lightsaber ignited, was the fearsome dark lord of the Sith himself. The sound of his mechanical wheezing filled the compartment as he stared down at me menacingly.

"At last you have come," he began. "I've been waiting for you. None of your crew seemed to be up to the challenge of beating me in comba —"

RRRIIIIIIINNNNGGGGGG

My world shifted. No longer was I tactical cyborg AM-75 facing off against Darth Vader in the bridge of our starship; we were back at St. Theresa School, and recess had just come to an end. Coming up behind me was Drew, now firmly back in his role as my schoolyard friend. He smiled as he spoke, wiping a lock of thick black hair out of his face as we walked together.

"You really ran for it after I told you to!"

"Well, I wasn't about to let the ship get taken by the Empire, was I?"

"Don't act like you would have won," quipped Jason. He was shorter than me, with lighter hair and blue eyes. "My lightsaber could totally have blocked your missiles."

"Nu-uh."

"Uh-huh."

"Guys, I think we're all forgetting the doctor over here," interjected Saria. "I totally was about to help."

"Is that why I ran into the bridge alone?" I shot back teasingly, feeling like I was finally getting the hang of this schoolyard banter thing. She huffed indignantly.

"I was on my way. Was sneaking in the back way is all ..."

We laughed and made our way back to class. It had started with Saria asking me to play at recess but continued like this for months and then years afterwards. We were all of us imaginative kids who enjoyed living in fantasy worlds of our own creation, and recess provided us with a creative outlet for these impulses. Some of the best creative moments of my younger years were at school, second only to the imaginative play Mitch and I frequently engaged in. Freed from social constraints and in the presence of like-minded friends, my mind was free to wander and invent; and it did those and more.

Learning how to interact with my peers was a pivotal experience. I am an inherently shy and introverted person, and the social norms and rules which apparently come so naturally to many others didn't present themselves as obvious to me. People seemed to understand the rules better than I did, and I always kind of kept to myself as a result. Because of this, finding my place among friends at that tiny elementary school was one of the happiest things that happened to me as a kid. It's also telling that, as an adult, I've come to realize that almost everyone in that friend group has either been confirmed to be neurodivergent in some way (autism, ADHD, etc.), or suspects it about themselves. Again, we differently wired folks always seem to find our own.

In retrospect, I consider my time at St. Theresa to have been among my best school years. At the time, though, other social struggles were real. For every recess play time like the ones I shared with Saria, Drew, and Jason, there were other moments when, like most kids, I had a hard time. In my case, as someone on the autistic spectrum, I often had difficulty knowing when (and when *not*) to talk or how to contribute to discussions. One of my teachers and I even developed a kind of joking solution where she, while appreciating my spirit, had taken to correcting me with subtle "my way or the highway Adam!" jabs in class. While these often made us all laugh, the message wasn't lost on me, and I began to learn some of my most important social lessons. Some were more easily picked up than others.

§

When I was around ten, the Nintendo 64 was launched and kids everywhere were wild for it. The system was revolutionary for its time, with amazing 3D graphics and countless new games. And, right along with it came Nintendo's then-latest iteration in the Mario Kart franchise: *Mario Kart 64*. The commercial for the game involved a circus fun house, with carnival music in the background. For reasons beyond me, I became fascinated by it. I'm not quite sure if it was because of how desperately I wanted a Nintendo 64, or if it was something else entirely, but whatever the cause, I became obsessed with the tune. I found myself humming it constantly, even at school. Oddly, I began to revel in how annoyed I could make my classmates with it. I was enjoying it, so how bad could it really be?

Needless to say, no one in my class was all that impressed.

I eventually got the hint, of course, but not before I had thoroughly annoyed several of my fellow grade schoolers in the process. Eventually, the entire incident blew under the rug and life went on, but through that situation, I learned that oftentimes, even if I was enjoying something, it didn't mean everyone felt the same way. This wouldn't be the last time I would face such a situation, but it certainly helped me begin to find my footing with various social rules that didn't come instinctively to me. It wasn't until the next time it happened, however, that I would begin to internalize it.

§

"You haven't seen *Star Trek: First Contact*?" I asked incredulously. The other boy shook his head, not knowing what his "no" was getting him into. He was slightly sporty, though also quite bookish — definitely my kind of person. We had become fast friends at summer camp, though in retrospect I can't remember his name. We'll call him Jeremy.

"Jeremy it's amazing," I exclaimed, bouncing in my seat on the bus as it dropped us off at camp. I looked at him, my eyes wide with passion as I spoke.

"I've never really watched *Star Tr* —"

"It has cool action, and the Enterprise looks so cool. And the Borg are awesome. And Worf totally kicks butt."

"That's cool. I like Ac —"

"And there's this really awesome part where they almost blow up the ship, but they don't, because Picard has to go save Data from the Borg Queen."

This went on and on ... and as it did, Jeremy seemed less and less interested. He even lost the will power to feign interest, and his eyes just seemed to glaze over in boredom. I was too wrapped up in what I was excitedly rambling about to notice. After all, if I was interested, surely Jeremy would be too, right?

"I don't like *Star Trek* alright?" Jeremy finally snapped. The bus had stopped in the camp's parking lot, which worked out wonderfully, since he got up and stormed away from me. I was upset, but also confused. What had I done to deserve that reaction? We were just talking; he shouldn't be that angry.

When I got home from camp that night, I asked Trish about it. She stopped doing the dishes for a moment as if lost in thought, then looked down at me as she spoke.

"Well Adam, maybe he just wasn't interested in *Star Trek*."

"Well I *know* that," I replied. "He told me."

"Well just because you are really interested in something, doesn't mean everyone is," Trish explained. "Sometimes you need to give other people a chance to talk about the things they want to talk about too."

This sounds like common sense, but it was like a light came on in my brain, and I was suddenly privy to a secret stash of information that only a select few are aware of. That's very much the thing about having a place on the autism spectrum: once something is pointed out to us, we're usually the first people to take note. I felt bad for boring Jeremy, but at the same time, I'd genuinely had no idea I had. Not until I had it pointed out to me that is.

Psychologists have traditionally referred to this as *theory of mind*, and it's commonly understood to be one of those things that doesn't develop in the same way for those of us on the autism spectrum. It's not even necessarily something that's *impaired* in the autistic brain (though psychologists coming at it from a neurotypical perspective *might* try to argue that ...) as much as it is something that works differently. Most fellow autistics I've met can communicate quite effectively with each other for example, it's only when we try to do so with non-autistics that we run into problems. My one-sided conversation with Jeremy about *Star Trek*? In the autistic community, that's known as *info-dumping*, and is actually considered an honour, as it means someone likes you enough to share one of their favourite things. It's commonly expected in such circles that you return the favour too. Naturally, this isn't how non-autistic people do things though, and hilarity often ensues as a result.

For this reason, I've observed that the autistic community as a whole doesn't tend to feel the traditional understanding of theory of mind goes far enough because it ignores the fact the communication breakdown actually goes both ways. Because of this, the term *double empathy problem* is preferred. It was coined by autistic researcher Damian Milton and refers to the nature of autistic-neurotypical communication as being more of a two-way street. Both sides struggle to understand each other, and I've had this proven true to me in my own life more times than I can count.

CHAPTER 6

"I won't play you for keepsies!" Dean and I stared at each other; our eyes locked. In the late 90s, marbles had become *the* game at St. Theresa's. Naturally it soon developed into the schoolyard equivalent of high-stakes gambling — at least, for most kids. To me, it was really more of a video game side quest — a diversionary activity which had the potential for big winnings ... and even bigger defeats. I was torn; I wanted to earn the schoolyard fame and prestige that came with winning such an intense match with Dean (not to mention some primo marbles), but not at the expense of losing some of my own in the process. My mother had only just given me my current set and I couldn't bear to see them go.

"What's the matter," Dean pushed. "Are you afraid?"

That was it. Being accused of not being able — or willing — to do a thing wasn't something I'd ever taken well, and I wasn't about to start then. Unfortunately, the trouble with being on the autistic spectrum is the ease with which people are able to manipulate you. Dean had me right where he wanted: riled up and reckless. If his goal was to get me to jump in and face him? Well, he should have seen how many hours I had spent replaying the penguin race level in *Super Mario 64*, determined to win. I didn't like to lose, and I wasn't about to let him have the last laugh.

"I am not afraid," I said at last, overcome by stubborn pride. As Dean smirked at me, I made my way over to the playing area, marble bag clutched in hand. Looking down, I undid the ties and took out my prized ball; a polished black marble that gleamed in the sun and had vibrant orange patterns dancing over its surface. I smiled at my challenger as he walked over.

"I bet I can beat you with this one here," I said, lifting my marble. Dean grinned.

"Oh really," he said, folding his arms across his chest. "Well then how about winner takes all. What do you say?"

By that point, I was in too deep. I accepted. We set to work playing, the objective being to use your own marbles to knock those of your opponent out of the small circle drawn — haphazardly in this case — in the schoolyard sand.

This should be a piece of cake, I reasoned to myself. My confidence certainly wasn't in short supply, and if there's one thing I've always excelled at, it's running head-first into things without thinking.

While I started the game doing well — I had knocked out a few of Dean's marbles and was quite proud of myself — it wasn't long before I lost my tenuous lead and my overconfidence evaporated with it. Dean gained the advantage, knocking several of my marbles out. If I didn't do something fast, I would lose and forfeit any stones I had used. I couldn't bear the thought and threw myself into winning. I lined up the perfect shot, guaranteed to knock almost every one of his marbles out if I pulled it off. Armed with arrogance and desperation, I let fly my orb and watched with bated breath, hoping beyond hope my last-ditch effort would succeed.

It did not.

Something that's important to remember about being autistic is this; you don't always know how to lose gracefully. You tend to want things your way, and to ignore the fact that sometimes in life, the universe deals you a crappy hand. This is precisely what happened during that ill-fated game of marbles, and unfortunately for my younger self, he lacked the socialization I now rely on to deal with such situations. To say I threw a fit would be putting things mildly.

"That's not fair," I yelled, feeling my face warm. "I could have gotten that shot!"

"It was a fair game man," Dean replied, looking taken aback by my reaction. "Don't be a cry baby about it; you lost fair and square."

My eyes welled up as a horrible sinking feeling engulfed me. I had just lost all the marbles Mom had bought me, and the thought made me feel sick.

No, I thought. *I can't let this happen; I have to get them back.*

Tears leaking from my eyes, I ran off toward the school, desperate to find a teacher — any teacher — willing to help. Finally, I found Madame Myer sitting at her meticulously organized desk, grading assignments then placing each marked sheet neatly in a stack to her left. My heart skipped a beat as I paused in the door. She was stern, but she was usually good for ending bullshit in its tracks. I approached her cautiously, like a wild animal.

"Madame," I began, heart pounding. She looked down at me and smiled.

"Adam? Shouldn't you be out at recess? The bell hasn't rung yet."

"Well ... it's just ... I lost my marbles and I need you to get them back."

She frowned, I think trying to figure out exactly what I meant. I wasted no time, rambling on trying to explain. Finally, Madame Myer pursed her lips, and interrupted my verbal stream of consciousness.

"So, you played marbles with Dean?"

"Yes, and he took mine from me when I lost."

"I see," she continued. "And, before you started playing, you agreed on the rules of the game?"

"Yeah, but —"

"And you said you'd play for keeps?"

"Well yeah ... but ..."

Shaking her head, Madame Myer leaned over her desk, bringing her face closer to mine. She sighed as her eyebrows furrowed.

"Well then there's nothing I can really do about this. You lost fair and square, and Dean won your marbles."

"NO!" I cried, the tears streaming now. "I just got those. I can't lose them. I can't."

Madame Myer handed me a tissue and knelt to my level. She smiled sympathetically and put a hand on my shoulder as I took the tissue and blew my nose.

"I know it's not fun," she began. "But it's part of life. If you agree to play a game by certain rules, then you need to accept the consequences if it doesn't go the way you wanted it to. Do you understand?"

But it's not fair, I remember thinking, my tears and snot soaking the Kleenex as I bawled. Eventually, the waterworks calmed, and with a sniffle I composed myself and looked back up at Madame Myer.

"Yes Madame," I mumbled at last.

"You're a good boy Adam," she said. "I know it's not always easy for you when you don't get what you want, but someday you'll understand better why lessons like these are important. Now run along, you still have five minutes of recess left."

I nodded, feeling better, and ran back out to join my friends in the schoolyard.

With the 20/20 hindsight vision afforded by adulthood, Madame Myer's words make a lot of sense. It's almost as though I have an itinerary for how I'd like things to go and when they don't, disappointment ensues. As a child, this could easily push me to tears. I suppose it's the curse of being a sensitive soul too, but in general children on the spectrum don't deal with unexpected circumstances like these well. What I learned from Madame Myer that day was that I had to think carefully before getting myself into certain social situations, since I needed to balance ambition for success with how I would cope if things didn't go as expected. I'd be lying if I said I've conquered this;

the fact is I still get annoyed easily if, for example, Tim Hortons is out of the exact kind of bagel I want (Maple French Toast with double the plain cream cheese because they never give you enough unless you ask for too much). It's something I work on day by day.

In most video games, side quests and minigames help you level up your character, and as I left Madame Myer's room to go back out to recess, it occurred to me that perhaps, I had done a little levelling up too.

§

Even though Dr. Miller and her Ritalin had helped me begin to process my emotions regarding Trish and the divorce, we were still a long way from being out of the jungle. In fact, Trish and I continued to do battle for years. After all, emotions don't just disappear, and her strict approach to parenting also remained, causing us both no shortage of grief and anguish as it clashed with my autistic traits. For those of you familiar with Jumanji, no one had yet rolled a 5 or 8 in the cosmic board game that was my life, and so in the thick of things we both remained. The night I got home from school after playing keepsies with Dean, my attempt to explain to Trish what had happened devolved into a fierce melee between us over the silliest of things, asparagus.

"You are living under my roof, so you *will* do what I tell you to."

The battle lines had been drawn an hour earlier. The argument was trivial, but it had completely eradicated the day's marbles drama from my conscious mind. I refused to eat my asparagus. I hadn't tried it of course. I didn't want to. It languished on my plate, taunting me with its sickly green colour, utterly revolting bumpy texture, and a stench that instantly set off my gag reflex. If the whole ordeal had been a Pokémon battle from old Game Boy games, the asparagus would have just used some kind of sensory attack to disable me utterly. It would then have unfolded something like this:

Adam used DEFIANCE.

"I won't eat it." I screamed. Trish scowled.

Opponent TRISH used IMPASSIONED PLEA.

"Adam, your father and I work hard to put food on this table for this family and you *will* eat what we serve you. We can't go making special dishes because you refuse to even try something."

Her words, despite their logic, enraged me. She just didn't get it. The asparagus overloaded three of my senses all at once! I couldn't handle it. It needed to be off my plate, out of my life. Of course, I also didn't know how to explain any of this. I was only nine, I was overwhelmed, and I hated confrontation as much as I hated the asparagus. As such, I lashed out instead, responding in the only way I was capable of in that exact moment — with the big guns.

Adam used HURTFUL COMMENT.

"You're not my real mom anyway."

I was trembling as the words came out of my mouth. I regretted them instantly. After all, in every fight, there's always a point when one or both parties involved inadvertently pass the point of no return.

Trish and I had reached that point.

It was SUPER-EFFECTIVE.

Opponent TRISH became CONFUSED ...

My stepmom sat there quietly. The hurt, reflected in her expression, left her speechless. I was too agitated to care. We had just driven so rapidly past any sense of rationality that it was little more than a tiny speck in the metaphorical rear-view mirror. I would have done anything to win.

Opponent TRISH used OUTRAGE.

"How dare you speak to me like that?" Trish shot back at last, glaring at me from across the table. My father, for his part, merely sat there, completely bewildered.

Bystander DAD used BANISH.

"Go to your room."

We sat in complete silence for an excruciating moment. Dad

angry. Trish hurt. The asparagus mockingly triumphant. Finally, my fury cut through the heavy tension suspended in the air all around us.

"Fine!"

Adam FLED from the battle ...

Stomping up the stairs, rage filled me as I slammed the door and flopped onto my bed. In no time at all, the rage became sobbing. On some level, I knew it was a silly fight, but that wouldn't stop me from being stubborn about it all the same.

I resented everything about that night: having my story about the marbles-incident derailed before I even had a chance to tell it; being forced to do my homework as soon as I got home from school; being served a dinner I didn't like and not having my preferences taken into account; and worst of all, being told what to do by that impostor. Because no, I hadn't quite finished working out my feelings about Trish just yet.

Eventually, my anger subsided. I realized that, while I still had no intention of trying the vile asparagus (ew), my behaviour had been terrible. Between Dr. Miller's efforts and those of my mom, I'd begun to learn how to self-soothe, and once I'd taken a few deep breaths, I found myself able to think a bit more clearly. I really did want to get along with Trish, so with that in mind, I descended the stairs to apologize and move on.

I slowly shuffled my way from the base of the stairs and through the kitchen, approaching the living room door like a whimpering dog with its tail between its legs, ready to admit defeat. Crossing the threshold, I neared the dark blue recliner where Trish sat illuminated by the harsh light of the TV. In the background, a serious-looking news anchor was droning on about global affairs — a topic I was far too young to know much about. Noticing me, Trish muted the TV and looked over.

I mustered my courage, bit my tongue, and muttered, "I'm sorry ... Mum."

"You're sorry?"

I nodded.

"Yeah ... I'm sorry."

Sometimes, even Trish realized she may have overstepped her bounds and apologized back. Those were the best times.

"Well, I'm glad to hear it. Your behaviour was uncalled for. Your father and I just wanted you to eat your dinner."

"Yeah ... I know ..." Clearly, it wasn't going to be one of those times.

"And we work so hard to provide and make dinner. You don't get to tell us you don't like what's served."

"I know ... but ..."

"But what?" She cut in. "It's just so frustrating when we get into these productions over things like
this."

As Trish's lecture continued, I found myself getting upset all over again. I'd approached her with the intent of apologizing — of making peace. Any reasonable person would have sat down and talked things over instead of launching back into it, wouldn't they? Faced with this, I could only keep my newfound cool for so long. Trish didn't seem to notice though; she just kept talking and talking until the rage building inside me reached my gag reflex in much the same way the putrid scent of the offending asparagus had. Finally, I exploded again.

"Would you SHUT UP?" I screamed.

"Excuse me, but I was talking to you."

"I said I was sorry!" I shot back, a fresh rush of anger filling me.

"Well," parried Trish, "It doesn't sound like you're very sorry to me."

"I am," I screamed, "But you just keep going on and on and on."

"That's very rude." She stood from her chair and furiously motioned at the door, eyes bulging. "Go back to your room; you're grounded for a week."

Glaring up at her, my nine-year-old body shaking with rage, I stomped off, but not before one last jab. The finishing blow.

"FINE. I HATE YOU!"

§

Much like any Pokémon battle in the old games, the asparagus incident was only one of many between my parents and I. In fact, the dinner table frequently became our household's version of the Indigo Plateau. It was where all of our fiercest confrontations were waged, whether or not any of us wanted it to be. It wasn't that I didn't *want* to be good and have a good relationship with my folks, I just felt that I *couldn't*. Yes, I had committed to trying to make things work with Trish, but whenever I attempted to do things the way she decreed instead of how I wanted to, it was as though an intense wave of emotional and near-physical pain washed over me. Forcing myself to sit still and focus on my homework immediately after I got home from school, for example, hurt immensely. The same was true of eating foods like asparagus that disagreed with my senses. It's difficult to describe exactly what this felt like, except to say that it was like slamming my brain against a brick wall no one could see but me. Trish and my dad could only perceive defiance and argumentativeness, but internally, it was more akin to intense agony. I couldn't do the thing, and any effort they made to punish my behaviour just made me resent them all the more.

Of course, while we never made it much further than that in terms of actually addressing my sensory and focus issues at home, there was one way in which my parents gave me the tools to at least start to develop the self-confidence I needed to solve them for myself.

They put me in cadets.

CHAPTER 7

People often joke about sending misbehaved kids to some sort of military academy in order to get them to shape up. While this is usually an idle threat, I sort of ended up sending myself in 1998. Things at school were generally progressing well; Saria, Drew, Jason, and I (along with some others) were hanging out, getting close, and having fun at recess doing things like trading *Pokémon* cards and playing in our made-up worlds. Things on the street were also decent, with Mitch and I doing what we always did: creative play, gaming, and watching cartoons. Overall, I had the beginnings of a great little elementary school existence.

Except on the home front. Things were always more complicated on the home front.

Even after Ritalin and several sessions with Dr. Miller, Trish and I were no closer to making peace with each other. Her approach just wasn't working for me, and we each escalated the other as a result. "Bad" behaviour like this is almost always a symptom of deeper needs going unmet, and that was most definitely true for me back then. I was fighting hard against 'executive dysfunction' — a fun thing my brain did where it wouldn't let me do something I needed to do, no matter how much I knew it needed doing. I also didn't feel listened to, and all too often the focus was placed solely on how "appropriate" my actions were instead of on actually listening and communicating with me. To be fair to Trish, she was thrown into motherhood with little-to-no experience when she married my dad, so you can imagine how doubly difficult it was for her to now be mothering a ten-year-old boy on the autism spectrum who was going through his own pretty intense things.

Enter my friend Brian. His parents were both involved in our local branch of the Cadets Canada program, focused on providing kids with learning opportunities, structure, and discipline through a pseudo-military organization. When the time came for him to join the Navy League Cadets (as both of his older brothers had done before him), he eagerly asked me to join with him.

"Come on, it'll be cool!" Brian pleaded. "You'll get to do all sorts of cool stuff like play an instrument, and march, and wear a uniform, and learn things."

"A uniform?" I asked. I had always thought army stuff was cool as a kid, I loved learning anything new, and it sounded like a lot of fun. Of course, my young autistic brain wasn't fully processing what joining Cadets would mean, but Brian made it sound amazing. Regardless, my social anxiety poked through and reared its ugly head.

"I don't know Brian," I interrupted, as he yammered on about the uniform. "There are going to be lots of people there I don't know ..."

"Ask your parents then," he said. "But I think it'll be great."

And ask my parents I did. I don't think it's too surprising to hear they were overjoyed about my interest in Cadets. They probably figured the discipline would help my attitude, and that it would give me a place to work on my social skills. Mostly, I think they were just happy to have me out of the house a couple nights a week.

"I think it's a great idea," Trish exclaimed.

"Definitely. It'll be a good experience for you Adam," my dad said. Sitting across the dinner table from them, I raised an eyebrow quizzically.

"You guys really think so? I won't know anyone ..."

"But that's how you make new friends," said Trish. "Remember your first day at St. Theresa? You were nervous then too, right?"

I nodded, mulling the whole thing over. The thought of doing something like Cadets did seem cool; I'd always been jealous of the (albeit short) time Mitch had spent in Scouts. Plus there was the cool uniform. Resolved, I looked back up at Trish and my dad.

"Alright," I said at last. "I'll do it."

"Great," said Trish. "Herc, go call the O'Hares and let them know Adam will go with Brian."

"Just a sec," my dad said as he poured himself a cup of coffee. Trish looked at him and smiled, but in a way that meant business.

"Now Herc, I don't want them to be kept waiting. Adam told Brian he'd ask us," she appealed.

"Alright, alright." My dad huffed as he made his way to the phone. It was always this way between them; to borrow an extremely gendered and slightly problematic saying, Trish definitely wore the pants in their relationship. The two of them bickered frequently, but always out of love.

"Yeah, perfect thanks Libby." My dad said, hanging up.

"Brian's mom will pick you up on Friday nights at five to go to Cadets Adam ... but this first week, I'll drive you because she needs to do a few things beforehand. You and Brian will be starting together it looks like. Afterwards she'll drop you off at your mom's for the weekend."

"Well Adam," said Trish, smiling. "Looks like you're in the navy now!"

§

My first day in the Navy League was an interesting experience. For starters, I was late. I forget why exactly, but as I stumbled into the Sudbury Armory building that night, I remember feeling anxious and unsure what to do. My dad and I made our way to the administration office along a catwalk above the main area, or "deck" below, and checked in. When we got there, we were met by a young thirty-something officer with cropped black hair and large circular glasses.

"You must be Adam," he began. "Or rather ... Cadet Mardero."

"I guess?"

"I'm Lieutenant Provos," he said, smiling. He looked at my dad and nodded.

"I can take it from here and show him the ropes. We're done at 21:00. That means 9:00 p.m. in civilian time." He winked down at me.

"Sounds good. You going to be alright Adam?" my dad asked.

I nodded and smiled nervously. As enthusiastic as I'd been when Brian pitched this idea, the whole situation was starting to feel more and more foreign. *Was this really my kind of thing? What would this* really *do for me?* I had no clue, but for the moment? I was along for the ride.

Lieutenant Provos smiled again and led me out the door. We walked along the metal catwalk before descending a flight of stairs and walking rapidly across the large gym-like area he explained was called a "parade deck."

"Everyone's in class right now," he said. "In Navy League, you start at the rank of new entry, then progress to ordinary cadet, leading cadet, and finally to the petty officer ranks. Every level comes with things to learn and do, and once you get up to the petty officer ones, you get to be a leader yourself. All of the adult officers are in charge of different divisions, which are squads of cadets. I'm your officer since you're in the new entry squad, and we also have a cadet squad leader called a divisional petty officer, or DPO, who takes their orders from me."

It was a lot of information to absorb, but I followed along as best I could. *Me? A leader?* I had no idea what to think of that ... except that it might just be something I want to try. I decided at that exact moment that achieving a petty officer rank would be one of my goals in the program. I looked up at Lieutenant

Provos.

"I think I might want to try doing something like that, Lieutenant Provos, sir."

Provos looked down at me and grinned.

"Is that so? Well here's your first lesson then — I noticed you pronounced it *LOO-tenant*. That's the American way."

"I heard it pronounced that way on *Star Trek*, sir," I replied, surprised.

"I thought so," he said. "We get so much American content on TV these days. In Canada, we pronounce it the British way: *LEF-tenant*. Or *LUF-tenant*. They both sound basically the same. But you have to put an *F* where there isn't actually one."

Learning something new already? About the historical origins of language? I couldn't help but smile.

"And here we are," Lieutenant Provos said as we arrived at a steel door leading into one of the building's classrooms. "This is the new entry orientation class. They'll explain everything better than I could."

"Thank you, sir," I replied. He smiled and nodded as he opened the door for me. I saw Brian sitting inside and suppressed the urge to wave.

"Good luck, Cadet Mardero. Who knows? You may just be my divisional petty officer some day."

§

The Cadet program really did what they could to help (or maybe force) recruits to overcome their anxieties. In that initial orientation class, we went over the things Lieutenant Provos had already explained, along with some new things. Uniforms, for example, were not issued until six weeks in. This was to ensure those who wore the uniform actually earned it and wanted to be there. In addition to the basic divisions, there were two specialized ones — the Band and the Guard. The Band, of course, played music and tended to attract all the musically inclined cadets, while the Guard carried replica rifles and did a unique form of drill involving them. Both competed at province-wide competitions. If we're being honest? Band sounded infinitely more fun.

After what felt like no time at all in the new entry orientation class, we were ushered back out to the deck and told to form up into our noobie division — a squad I soon learned was called *Chicoutimi* (an Indigenous word, though I didn't know that at the time). It all happened extremely fast, and I felt like a fish out of water. I had never once done military drill in my life, and not long after we fell in, I learned that the concept of not being able to move while at attention was much harder to follow through with in practice than I expected it to be. My feet ached, my body craved movement, and just when I thought learning basic parade drill couldn't get any worse, my nose started to itch. But I couldn't scratch it. But not being able to just made me want to all the more.

ARGH!

We'd been out of class and formed up on the parade deck for only a few minutes, but I was already starting to think the whole endeavour wasn't for me. Yes, leadership sounded fun, and yes, getting promoted inspired me, but was it really worth it? I wasn't sure, but then something happened that changed my view entirely; we started to march.

It's going to sound silly and suspiciously nationalistic (not to mention, extremely cringy in retrospect), but I felt a swirling of pride as I took part in something so impressive ... so awe-inspiring. It felt like I was part of a well-oiled machine, and while I had much to learn — where marching and doing drill properly were concerned — I felt an eagerness to try. And so, dressed in nothing but 'civvies' (the internal Cadets term for 'regular clothes') and surrounded by the rest of my fellow noobies, I threw myself into it. We marched for roughly ten minutes, the band blaring all manner of catchy military music, the entirety of our cadet corps of forty moving as one. It stirred something in me.

With just a little marching, I wanted to better myself, work hard, and rise as high in the cadet ranks as I could. *I'm going to do it*, I thought to myself as we finished the march and came back to attention. *I'm going to be a petty officer someday. I'm going to get the highest rank I can.*

For a kid like me, who so often struggled with time management, knowing how to relate to others, and emotional regulation, Navy League Cadets became a perfect outlet for me to learn ambition, structure, self-discipline, and leadership skills. These were areas in which I definitely needed a safe space to practice, and Cadets provided that.

§

The next few months in the Cadets program saw me grow more comfortable in my own skin and develop a sense of responsibility; I joined the Guard, learned specialized rifle drill, and even started attending weekly practices every Sunday in addition to the regular Cadet meets on Friday nights. It felt good to be part of something like that, but I would be lying if I said it was always easy or a good fit. In fact, sometimes, it bordered on overwhelming.

One of the ways Cadets overwhelmed me as a neurodivergent person was in terms of opportunities for downtime. Like most autistic people, I had a limited reservoir of emotional energy, and Cadets frequently siphoned more than its fair share. Between going to school every day and then Cadets every Friday night and Sunday afternoon, it's safe to say I felt like I wasn't getting enough time to myself. Everyone except my mom underestimated just how much I needed down time, and that didn't help much because I only saw her every second weekend.

By the end of Friday night Cadet meets, I was burned out. I'd go home — either to my dad and Trish's, or to mom's — and immediately collapse on my bed. Taking off my boots was like putting out a raging inferno that had taken hold on the aching soles of my feet. Likewise, changing out of my uniform was like shedding a hellishly uncomfortable carapace. The collar of the shirt was just a tad too tight; the pants were made of a material that itched, and the hat constricted my head in a very unpleasant way that didn't seem to bother anyone else but me. I yearned for my body to be free of the sensory hell the outfit represented, and it felt heavenly to throw my pyjamas on once my Cadet uniform had been removed.

On weekends when I was at my mom's, I'd often wind down after Cadet night by playing video games or watching *Star Trek* with her before climbing into bed. If I was really lucky, she'd sometimes take me to Blockbuster to rent a Nintendo 64 game on our way home from the Sudbury Armory. Saturdays would pass far too quickly, and be filled with either time spent with Mitch, or adventures my mom would take me on around town during my times with her. Sundays would, of course, be consumed by Guard practice from 12-4; an intense day of drill, marching, and even more physical discomfort.

In effect, I only had one day off per week. If this sounds exhausting, I can assure you that to me as an autistic person, it was hell. I was rapidly growing tired of feeling as though I had no time to myself, and I missed Mitch too. We spent time together when we could, but it just wasn't the same. During one weekend sleepover, he expressed to me how much he too longed for the old days.

"Don't you ever get tired of it?" Mitch asked me late one Saturday night. We had built blanket forts in his basement and had stayed up late, with only the light of our flashlights and the full moon shining in through the big bay window nearby to guide us. I looked over at him and sighed.

"All the time," I replied honestly. It wasn't that I didn't like aspects of being in Cadets, simply that the sheer amount of time I spent there had really begun fraying my nerves. "But what can I do? I have to do it. I'm already in it."

"I get that," Mitch answered. "But I miss my best friend too. I feel like I never see you anymore. At least, not as much on the weekends. And those were always our best hangouts."

"I know," I sighed again. I missed him too. I missed being a normal kid and not having to go to regular Cadet meets on Friday nights and Guard practices on Sundays. They were exhausting days filled with discipline and drill and combined, they pushed my body and mind to their limits.

"But hey," I finally said, "at least we can still see each other every other day when I'm not at Cadets. You can't get rid of me that easily."

§

My conversation with Mitch that one fateful night had stuck with me, and I found myself unable to ignore my strong feelings of autistic overwhelm after that. There came a point when the intensity finally got to me. I had enough; I was burned out. And so, on a fateful Sunday afternoon while at Guard practice, I made my move. I marched up to Midshipman Obanson, the officer in charge of the Guard squad, and expressed my desire to quit. I was terrified, but also fed up with the feeling that Cadets had taken over my life.

"Midshipman Obanson, sir?"

"Yes, Mardero?" He looked me over. "What can I do for you?"

"Sir, I think I want to quit. It's not that I don't appreciate everything you and Lieutenant Provos and the others have done for me, but I'm just not having a lot of fun with Cadets anymore."

"I understand," he replied. It was practice, so neither of us were in uniform, but he still carried himself with proper military stiffness. "Well naturally I won't try to stop you. But you're a good cadet and member of the Guard ... and you've come a long way in a short time. I'd hate to lose you. You should at least talk to your parents about it after practice tonight."

"I can do that," I nodded. As requests went, I didn't think this one would be that big of a deal. After all, surely my mom, dad, and Trish would also understand and be okay with my decision.

Spoiler alert: they didn't and they weren't. At least they never let on they felt otherwise.

"You did what?" Trish and my dad were both in shock. Neither of them expected me to do something like that, and when they found out they both put their feet down.

"Well, you're not quitting," my dad ordered in a style reminiscent of the stifling military environment I was attempting to leave behind. "You're going to go back there and tell them you changed your mind."

"But I haven't changed my mind."

"Oh yes you have!" Trish shot back. "You can't just quit Adam; you made a commitment."

I couldn't believe it. Why couldn't they see I was miserable? Cadets was too much and I hated it.

"Adam, I agree with Trish," my mom reluctantly said later that night when I called to complain. "A commitment is like a promise, and what did I always teach you about promises?"

"That you can't break them," I replied. "But —"

"No buts Adam," my mom interjected. "I know you can't see it now, but trust me, years from now, you'll look back on this and be glad we didn't let you quit."

"I don't see how ...," I grumbled.

"I know," my mom responded casually. I could almost hear her infuriating smile on the other end of the phone. "But you will."

And so, I didn't quit Cadets ... not that day anyway, though I did end up switching from the Guard to the Band and having a *far* better experience. Learning to play a musical instrument was way more fun (even if it was only the crash cymbals in the percussion line) and I really came to enjoy the creative outlet of putting on impressive marching band performances with my peers at provincial competitions every year. I'd found my niche, and for a time anyway, things got more manageable. They were even — dare I say it — fun.

Before long, I found myself rising in the ranks. First came Ordinary Cadet (OC — the first rank after the basic New Entry level), then Able Cadet (AC), then Leading Cadet (LC), and finally Petty Officer Second Class (PO2).

Or it would, provided I passed the exam to achieve it.

Every rank in Cadets came with an examination designed to verify we had the skills necessary to warrant the promotion, and PO2 was no different. Except of course, to me. It was the rank I had aspired to since my first night in the program, and now it was almost within reach. I crammed hard, studying the Cadet handbook and preparing myself in every way I knew how before Friday night inevitably rolled around. That Cadet night, instead of going to class like usual, we were taken to write our promotion exams.

I took my seat at a long brown cafeteria-style table along with the rest of my cohort of LC cadets, each of us spaced six feet apart to prevent cheating. Lieutenant Hughs — a large, physically imposing man who is rumoured to have served in the actual military and certainly looked the part — handed out our exams.

This was it. The moment of truth. I picked up my pencil as soon as I could and began filling things out. School had always come relatively easily to me after all, and this was just school-like enough for that to be a transferable skill. After about half an hour, I'd completed the test as best I could, handed it in to Hughs, and headed to the parade deck for Canteen time. There was a Grape Crush with my name on it, and after all that? I was ready for a break.

A few weeks later, I got the news. That night, at the end of the regular Cadet meet, they ended early and started calling out names of cadets who were to report to the front dais while we all stood at attention. It was standard procedure for promotion nights, and my heart nearly stopped as I heard my name.

"LC Mardero."

Grinning with pride, I stepped forward, crisply put my instrument down, and marched to the front of the parade deck. Standing before us was the Commanding Officer of Navy League Cadet Corps Sudbury — an older woman with a demeanour of steel who we knew as CO Larabie. She walked down the line, handing each of us a rank insignia until she reached me. She stopped, our eyes making uncomfortable contact for a moment as I stood at attention.

"Mardero," she acknowledged.

"Ma'am," I replied crisply, knowing not to speak out of turn. Larabie nodded.

"You came to us rather haphazardly, didn't you?" I could almost see a grin forming on her face, but it was so subtle that I wasn't sure. Her comment confused me, and I answered the only way I knew how.

"Ma'am?"

"Your first night, cadet. You stumbled in here late, and I had to pull Lieutenant Provos away from his duties just to make sure you got to class. You also tried to quit within the first six months of being here. Does that seem professional to you, cadet?"

My heart sank. As ever, I seemed to always take two steps back for every step I took forward. Would my disorganized first night and attempt to quit never be forgotten?

"No, CO Larabie, ma'am."

"That's right it's not. It's sloppy and disorganized. I noticed it about you right away. But do you know what else I noticed?"

My heart stopped as I braced for the worst.

"Your tenacity and determination. Lieutenant Provos told me about the conversation he had with you that first night. We were both extremely impressed by your intelligence and desire to achieve a Petty Officer rank. I was also personally impressed when you came back after telling Midshipman Obanson you wanted to quit. It takes a lot of guts to admit you're wrong and to stick with something you know is hard, wouldn't you say?"

"Yes Ma'am." I was not prepared for the way this conversation had gone. At first, I thought Larabie was getting ready to boot me out of the program. Now it seemed she was ... praising me?

"Indeed it does. Which is why tonight, I'm not only going to promote you. You passed your exam with flying colours and earned that much. But you've also demonstrated growth, strength of character, and development unlike any other cadet here. You overcame your own anxiety and rose to the challenge of being here despite struggling more against the structure of the program than anyone else in your year. And because of *that*, I'm also awarding you the distinction of 'Most Improved Cadet.'"

I felt light as a feather. I couldn't believe it. Was this real? Was it happening? If I had been allowed to move, I'd have pinched myself to make sure I wasn't dreaming.

"Th-thank you CO Larabie, ma'am!" That time, I saw her grin for sure.

"You're welcome, *Petty Officer* Mardero."

§

After being promoted, I soon went on to become Divisional Petty Officer of *Chicoutimi* under Lieutenant Provos himself. He was extremely proud of me for that accomplishment, and my final year of Navy League proved to be my best one in the entire program. Getting to pass on my knowledge and experience to the New Entry cadets under my command felt empowering, but being a leader came with its own learning curve. Importantly, I came to understand a leader should never ask their people to do something they themselves aren't willing to do. Something like, say, putting your division on report and making them stand at attention during Canteen time if you don't also plan to stand on report with them ... a lesson I learned the hard way when I did so and then attempted to go buy a pop for myself while the rest of *Chicoutimi* went without. Needless to say, Lieutenant Provos was less than impressed.

But I digress. Earning that promotion and becoming DPO of *Chicoutimi* was a mostly positive experience and a great way to end my time in Navy League. All good things eventually come to an end though, and years later in 2003, I finally did quit Cadets. By that point, I had 'aged out' of (gotten too old for) Navy League and moved on up to its bigger sibling, Sea Cadets. That program wasn't nearly as beneficial for me, and really began to illustrate that perhaps I'd reached an impasse with the whole thing. I was 14, and teenage hormones, coupled with my own social challenges in middle school (more on that later), began to make Cadets harder and less rewarding. The officers joked around with us in weird, almost hurtful ways that the other kids didn't seem to mind, but I could never tell if they were serious or not. I wouldn't have admitted it at the time, but Asperger's had reared its head, and the whole situation bothered me more than I let on. Mostly, I just didn't find I was getting anything from the program anymore, and my own rapidly developing social conscience and interest in history had led me to start questioning many things about Cadets that I'd long taken for granted.

All things considered, Trish, my mom, and my dad each conceded that the time had finally come, and I turned in my notice not long after. As we brought back my uniform, I found myself lost in thought about the whole thing. Navy League Cadets had actually ended up being one of the best experiences of my young life. Despite the diminishing returns I'd felt by the time I got to Sea Cadets, I also came to understand exactly what my parents meant, and why they didn't let me quit all those years before. Commitments carried weight after all, and that was a lesson I internalized during my time there.

CHAPTER 8

Outdoor adventures are almost a rite of passage for most Northern Ontario kids, me included. It was the summer of 2000 — Y2K and Grade 6 were both safely behind me, and a new PlayStation was my obsession. Most importantly, though? My mom was taking me camping for the first time.

I had a complicated relationship with the outdoors, and it was definitely one of the aspects of being autistic I had the hardest time with growing up. It's not that I didn't appreciate the beauty of nature or the call of the wild — sunrises and sunsets by the water or over snow-crusted lakes have always been some of my favourite vistas — it's just that a lot of the things involved in spending time in the wilderness gave me anxiety. Leaves and dirt particles floating on a body of water I was about to go swimming in? No thanks. Walking through thick trees and having branches with all manner of contaminants brush through my hair, leaving unpleasant surprises in their wake? I'll pass. And then there were the leeches. It was autistic sensory hell. I still cringe when I think about it.

I had no idea how a character like Link survived a trek deep into a place like the Lost Woods or the bottom of Lake Hylia in various *Zelda* games, let alone a visit to Ganon's lair in the Dark World, but I knew there was no possible way I could handle it in my own life. Nature was something I enjoyed looking *at*, not being *in*. Why would I? Indoors, there was the computer, video games, TV, and air conditioning. The "great" outdoors on the other hand had bugs, mysterious specks of dirt, and disgusting creepy crawlies. And leeches. So many leeches.

Needless to say, I wasn't sold on how "great" the great outdoors could really be, but my mom wanted to change that. That summer, she decided to take me on an adventure to Manitoulin — a scenic freshwater island (the largest in the world) at the northern edge of Lake Huron. It's a popular tourist destination with several small, rural communities, six different First Nations, and a number of public and private campgrounds. The one my mom chose for that weekend was near M'Chigeeng First Nation and came recommended by friends with family in the area.

Neither of us could have known how that weekend would change us.

After an excruciatingly long and dull two hour drive down several extremely slow and boring northern highways surrounded by tall, dense trees and dotted by the occasional gas station and convenience store, we finally arrived on the island mid-afternoon. Immediately after we'd parked, we set to work pitching our tent on a flat, tree-covered plot of land not far from the campground's public bathrooms. This was one of those things that made me not like the outdoors — how do you stay clean? How do you ... you know ... relieve yourself? Thankfully, our proximity to the camp's amenities solved that particular problem.

"Hey sweetie," my mom called, looking over as she worked to secure her side of the tent. "When we're done here, did you want to go for a walk on the beach? I saw a really nice quiet area as we were coming in."

"Sure," I grunted, fighting with the pole I was trying to force into the ground.

"Great." My mom's eyes lit up. We finished up, threw our bags inside, and made for the beach.

Walking along the sandy shore of Lake Huron as the sun was beginning to set ... a question popped into my head that

I'd never thought to ask before. It was sudden, but I also felt I desperately needed it answered. When it appeared, I looked up at my mom, my face curling into a scowl.

"Why did you have to get divorced?"

My mom looked taken aback. She hadn't been expecting that question out of nowhere.

"What makes you ask that, Adam?"

"I don't know ... I'm just ... I'm sick of all of this. The whole thing!"

"Honey," my mom spoke softly, "you know I got sick. I couldn't take care of you and things got tough with your dad and me. It wasn't because I didn't love you ..."

"I know ... but ..."

"But what? Adam if you need to let something out, let it out. I promise I can take it."

The floodgates opened. The cork subconsciously (and rather imperfectly) bottling a hurricane of emotion deep within popped like a bottle of newly-opened champagne, and all my feelings came bursting out. Anger, sadness, terror, grief ... it had all finally been set free, and I let loose on the woman who gave me life.

"YOU LEFT ME WITH DAD AND TRISH! I CAN'T BELIEVE YOU LEFT ME WITH THEM. I'M ALL ALONE, AND NO ONE REALLY LISTENS TO ME, AND I'M TRYING SUPER HARD BUT TRISH AND I DON'T GET ALONG, AND DAD DOESN'T SAY ANYTHING, AND I JUST HATE IT!"

Without realizing it, I'd assumed an aggressive stance: my feet shoulder-width apart, my heart pounding as adrenaline coursed through my veins. My mom had taken a seat on a nearby rock, and her mouth hung open in surprise. A few tears fell from her eyes as she looked at me.

"Adam I ..."

"YOU WHAT?"

"I'm ... sorry ... I never meant to hurt you like this ... I just didn't think it would be good for you if I was around in those early years ... especially not while I was working through things with my therapist."

With that, my posture relaxed a little. My shoulders slumped and I exhaled. I was still livid, but the spike had passed.

"I know ... but I needed my mom ... I need my mom."

She reached her hand out as I inched closer. Grabbing it, I felt the anger vanish and a wave of sadness overtake me as I melted into her arms and sobbed.

"I know sweetie," she soothed, patting my back as I wept. "I am so sorry. I am such a terrible mother to you."

"No you aren't." I pulled my head back from its resting place on her shoulder and looked her straight in the eye. "You are an amazing mom. I love you so much."

"I love you too Adam. But I hurt you, and I hate that I did."

"It's not your fault," I argued, defending her from my own outburst. "You were sick, like you said. But I still need you. I always have, and I always will."

"I know you do," she said, pulling me deeper into the hug. "And I'm not going anywhere — I promise."

Overcome by emotions, I was barely able to speak, consumed by tears. I managed to look up at her one more time, and then hugged her even harder.

"I love you Mom. And I'm never leaving you either."

We spent the rest of the twilight hours sitting on the beach, holding each other as the sun set — both on the day, and on a great many complicated emotions I'd been carrying within for far too long.

The emotional dawn had finally come, and that day my mom had helped me regulate my big feelings in a way that not even Dr. Miller and Ritalin had. The monsters receded and the Hyrule Castle drawbridge descended.

I felt free at last.

§

It was dark by the time we finally made it back to our campsite. Not pitch black yet, but that lightish dark which exists immediately after the sun sets. Dinner consisted of a few cans of Alphaghetti and some crackers and cheese. Nothing too fancy, but processing a metric tonne of emotion has a way of making you hungry, and so I sat on the picnic table near our tent and ravenously consumed the processed tomato paste. In the distance, I could hear wolves howling as the moon shone brightly in the clear night sky. My mom walked over from the cooler, can of spaghetti in hand. Smiling, she sat down across from me.

"You know Adam, after dinner, I want to show you something really special."

That had my attention. *What was she talking about now?*

"How would you like to go stargazing tonight? There's less light pollution out here, and I bet the view will be incredible."

I nodded enthusiastically, slurping down the last of my canned pasta. By the time we'd both finished eating, night was in full swing. Flashlights in hand, we made our way to a small clearing between our tent and the public washrooms. There was no one else around, the only sounds being the hum of bugs in the trees and the distant crashing of soft waves breaking on the shore. My mom smiled and pointed at the sky. "Look up, sweetie. I don't think you'll want to miss this."

Slowly, I tilted my head upward, and my jaw dropped. In the city, you might look up and see a few specks of light dotting the blackness of the cosmic canopy, but on Manitoulin that night, it was different. Mom was right; there was far less light pollution, and because of it the stars shone through clear as day.

Scattered across the black, cloudless sky the stars were a thousand pinpricks. Each the remnant of a time long ago. Each standing watch over its own unique solar system. Who knows? Maybe some of them even had their own Earth-like planets, and their own beings looking up into the endless night. Mom clearly saw how awestruck I was, and she moved over and placed her hands on my shoulders.

"I love you Adam. I'm glad we came camping this weekend."

I nodded in agreement. Being autistic often means feeling

everything more intensely, and in my case, while that definitely included the kind of emotions I had experienced earlier, it also encompassed having an almost child-like wonder at the mysteries of the universe. I was consumed by it. I've always loved the stars — astronomy, space, the universe, all of it. There's just something about the perpetual infinity they represent, and it made me think of how much I'd have loved to have been on a starship, cruising around amongst them.

Seeing them as I did that night struck me deeply to the core of my being.

Chapter 9

In middle school, I became obsessed with *Star Trek*. In many ways it was the lens through which I saw my world. The stars had always fascinated me, and I had also always been stubbornly consumed by a desire for fairness. *Star Trek* spoke to both of these inclinations, while also making me dream of all the promises of science and technology.

I was deeply invested, and it's a good thing too; Grades 7 and 8 were destined to be challenging years, and *Star Trek* rapidly became a source of comfort for me in the darkest of times. In the fall of 2000, I found myself thrown into the melting pot of middle school, away from my old group of friends, and struggling to fit in. Drew was a year younger than me, meaning he wouldn't be joining us until 2001, and while Saria did come along, middle school had a way of completely separating all of us as we quickly got sorted into different social cliques. This prospect would be terrifying enough for a non-autistic child, let alone an autistic one. The idea of blending with a hundred or so other students, being separated into various home rooms, and having to figure out where I fit into it all was intimidating and overwhelming to say the least. St. Francis was a massive, multi-story brown brick building that collected students from all over Sudbury's south end, and as I walked in the door for the first time, I knew I didn't belong.

I felt like an alien — a Starfleet officer cut off from the rest of his away team and forced to try to blend in with the locals (and not violate the Prime Directive — that sacred Starfleet general order that required all personnel to not reveal themselves to pre-contact civilizations) in order to survive. Thanks to an analytical personality — shaped by my autistic and ADHD brain — though, I soon found a new role for myself: cultural anthropologist. While I felt separated and unable to connect with my fellow classmates, I was also fascinated by their complex social structure. In any given situation, I could tell you all the details: the popular cliques all stood around in perfect circles at recess for some reason, they wore way too much Axe, the girls sometimes dyed their hair red. I could tell you who was popular, who wasn't, and who they all were, but I was always missing one key piece of the puzzle — how to fit in.

Don't get me wrong; I did *try* to fit in. I tried following their social rules as best I could understand them, and I tried cracking the jokes they seemed to laugh at. I even tried to engage them in conversation several times. The Universal Translator was either broken, or I'd misinterpreted their customs, because I may as well have been shouting "Darmok and Jalad at Tanagra" for all the good it did me.

That, or maybe they understood perfectly, and simply refused to accept me as one of their own for reasons only they knew. More study was definitely required.

§

Beyond the social isolation, there was some pretty overt bullying directed my way too. It took many forms, but the two main instigators who made my life difficult were Geo and Ritchie. They were the kings of the school yard if you will. Geo was a class clown with an attitude problem. He was a constant nuisance to all the teachers, always getting into fights, and the subject of more than a couple crushes. Ritchie shared some of these traits with Geo, but he was less likely to pick fights (he still tagged along with Geo whenever he started one though).

The two ran in the same crowd and capitalized on their seemingly innate likeability and capacity to make other kids laugh. It was an extrovert quality I didn't understand. None of my Starfleet training had prepared me for encountering it. I didn't know how it was possible for me to do the same things they did, and yet for it to not yield the same results. Scientifically, it made no sense. Experiments should be reproducible, yet middle school social rules didn't seem to work that way. They appeared to follow a logic all their own. This lack of comprehension often opened me up to the cruel manipulation of my peers.

§

"Hey Adam, that's a pretty cool book you've got there."

Ritchie stood at the base of the stairwell as I descended one day after class. My heart started pounding the minute I saw him. *What does he want?* I wondered as I inched steadily closer.

"Um ... thanks."

"Yeah. Sure. You're always reading, aren't you?"

"Well ... I mean I do like reading ..."

I had no idea why Ritchie was being so nice to me. Part of my brain kept screaming not to trust him, that something was wrong. Unfortunately, that part of my brain hasn't always been the loudest, and that day, my optimistic enthusiasm drowned it out.

"I see that. *Star Trek*, right?"

"Yeah. It's great," I confirmed, reaching the bottom of the stairs. *He really is interested.* I thought. Could I have changed Ritchie? Could Gene Roddenberry — creator of *Star Trek* — be right about it being possible for everyone to get along?

"I bet," Ritchie eyed my books as I went to pass him and move down the hall. Before I realized what was happening, his hand whipped out and flipped the books I was carrying out of my grip and they scattered all over the ground.

"Doing that is pretty great too," Ritchie chuckled. He grinned maliciously and made one last jab before turning to go to his locker. "Pick up your books. Nerd."

I slumped to the ground and fought back tears as I rushed to pick up my books. "Fake nice" was a phenomenon I'd noted in my field studies almost immediately, but I still struggled to differentiate it from legitimate niceness. I did, however, notice that it was becoming more and more common as a tactic used against me by a few of my classmates. They seemed to get some kind of sick thrill from it, such that eventually I came to exist in an almost constant state of "I know this is a trap but I don't know how." Having talked about this to many fellow autistic adults, I've come to realize that this was a bullying strategy many of us faced because of our difficulties reading social situations. When I was a kid though, it resulted in me pushing most people away before they even had a chance to show their true colours. Even though many people were probably genuinely trying to be nice, it was just easier to not trust anyone.

§

Despite my best attempts to either blend in with the cultural mores of the locals or avoid my classmates altogether, it was very apparent that I didn't belong among them. Because of this, Geo and Ritchie saw fit to make my life a living hell for the two years I spent at that school. All of a sudden, I started to wonder if perhaps there was something to the Asperger's thing after all. I was certainly struggling enough to understand my classmates, and school felt like a daily exercise in social frustration and ostracization. It was like they saw something in me that I didn't see in myself, and for whatever reason, they didn't like it.

The words of Dr. Jackson that I'd heard mockingly parroted back to me by my mom started swirling in my mind. It was a little like how Gaius Baltar in the Ronald D. Moore version of *Battlestar Galactica* was taunted by a version of Cylon Number 6 in his head that no one else could see. "Adam will never be able to form meaningful social connections," Head-Jackson said. "He will struggle in all things."

It didn't matter that Dr. Jackson never actually said that last part. My brain made it feel like he did, and I immediately got defensive.

No, I thought to myself. *There's nothing wrong with me. Dr. Jackson was wrong.*

But the thing was, I couldn't be sure of that. After all, I'd heard the word Asperger's tossed around a lot at home after my session with Sue. Only my mom had sat down and explained it to me, and even then, I didn't know much about it. I just knew it was something nebulous I'd been told I had. Somehow, it had to do with why I sometimes didn't understand other people, but that was all I really got from my parents on the subject.

Giving in to Jackson's words felt wrong though. They sounded ridiculous, so there was no possible way he was right about me. Asperger's sounded like a disability, and I certainly didn't *feel* disabled. I could walk and talk and get good marks at school and explain a temporal predestination paradox along with why you should never go back in time and marry your own grandmother in a system where time is linear (thank you, *Back to the Future* and *Star Trek*). I felt *normal,* more or less.

Sorry Dr. Jackson, I proclaimed internally, glaring intently at the manifestation of him my mind had cooked up. *But you are wrong.*

Even in that moment, I knew that was probably a lie I was telling myself. Asperger's could very well have been a factor in my struggles, but I wasn't yet ready to admit it. I wanted to stand stubbornly and try to face it all myself, without any help. Cadets had shown me the value of sheer force of will, and that was how I'd prove to the world I was just as capable as anyone. That I had the same right to exist as everyone else.

It was on me to crack the middle school social code. No one else could do it for me, and I'd be damned if I'd ask for any help with it either. I have to admire the dogged determination of my pre-teen/early teenage self. Despite it though, the bullying I faced persisted.

One lunch hour, for example, I was deeply engrossed in the classic *Star Trek* novel *Star Trek: Federation* and minding my own business when — *thwack!* — an orange hit me on the side of the head. When I looked up, I saw the culprit, Geo this time, grinning at me from across the room. Everyone around him was laughing hysterically. I felt tiny.

That's not to say I never stood up to them, mind you. After all, every good Starfleet officer has an obligation to stand up to injustice, and I for one knew my duty well. Jean-Luc Picard demanded nothing less; though once, doing so almost got me suspended. I was in Grade 8 by then, accustomed to their antics. We were standing outside the music classroom waiting for the teacher to usher us in. As usual, I was absorbed in my own little world — Mitch and I had just invented an awesome new sci-fi story, and we had started playing it out with LEGO because I had some great ideas for spaceship designs — when out of nowhere, Geo and Ritchie crept up from behind and startled me.

I jumped and yelled. My heart was racing; I was not expecting it. The whole class laughed. I got so angry when I realized what had happened that I spun around and attacked the two of them with all of the physical clumsiness of one of those wacky, waving inflatable tube men used in advertising. I tried to land a blow on Ritchie, but it became an awkward slap; when I tried to repeat the attack on Geo, I lightly scratched him instead. Physical coordination had never really been my thing, but it felt good to defend myself all the same.

Serves them right, I thought as they bolted, shocked I'd actually fought back.

"Adam Mardero to the principal's office."

My blood went cold as I heard the announcement on the school P.A. system. Part of me hadn't believed I'd get punished. After all, they'd done so much worse to me over the years!

Sitting in the office, I was terrified at the prospect of getting in serious trouble for my actions. *I'm not a bad kid,* I thought. *I don't deserve this.* The principal, Mr. Grassini, was a broad-built Italian man with short-cropped greying brown hair and a rather large nose protruding from his face, but he wasn't the one who held the real power ... at least, not among the student population. No, that honour went to Mrs. Laura MacDonnell, the vice principal — a tall, lanky woman with shoulder-length black hair hanging evenly from the top of her head. On her nose rested a pair of thin-rimmed spectacles, and she would not have looked out of place wearing a drill sergeant's uniform and a pair of sunglasses, chewing on a stalk of grass. I begged and pleaded with both of them not to be suspended, but my pleas fell on unsympathetic ears. They glared at me as I babbled.

"Do you know why you're here, Adam?" Mr. Grassini folded his arms and leaned across the desk. He furrowed his brow; they looked at me expectantly. I nodded, unsure how else to respond.

"Good," Mrs. MacDonnell spoke curtly. "Geo and Ritchie told me quite a story. Apparently, they walked up to you and said 'hi,' and you *attacked* them?"

My eyes went wide as I realized just what the two of them had told her.

"That's not true at all," I protested. "Well, it's *kinda* true ... but they started it! I —"

"Save it, Mr. Mardero," Mr. Grassini interjected. "We have a zero-tolerance policy at this school for any kind of violence. What you did definitely qualifies. I must say, this is extremely unexpected from you of all people, and I'd be lying if I said I wasn't disappointed. I'm going to be having a word with your parents tonight after school."

My heart sank to the very pit of my stomach when I heard that. I'm done for, I thought. I'll be suspended for sure, and when Trish finds out ...

Oh my God; when Trish finds out, I'll never see the light of day again.

§

That night, when Trish came in the door I was so worked up with anxiety that I ambushed her almost immediately.

"Mum ... I'm sorry ..." I said, bowing my head as she undid her shoes and hung up her jacket.

"What's wrong Adam?" She frowned. At that point, I couldn't help myself and I started rambling.

"It's ... these two guys at school. They attacked me and I attacked them and Mr. Grassini said he'd be calling you and —"

"Adam, did you get into a *fight*?" Trish scowled, but she couldn't hold it for very long before I started sobbing.

"I couldn't help it mum," I began, wiping tears away from my eyes as I tried desperately to explain. "You don't know what it's like. The other kids either bully me or they don't say anything when others do, and the teachers don't do anything about it, and no matter what I do, it doesn't stop."

Trish's scowl immediately disappeared, replaced with a frown as she pulled me in close and hugged me while I cried it out. Finally, she looked me in the eyes, a determined expression on her face. "What happened, Adam?"

And with that, I explained everything. I told her about Geo and Ritchie's bullying, about their near constant verbal attacks, about all the times I'd tried and failed to get them to stop — everything, culminating in that day's drama in line for music class. By the time I was done, I could barely keep back the tears. Almost as if by clockwork, the phone rang not long after.

Mr. Grassini was calling for my date with destiny. I shuddered, but Trish smiled sympathetically and uttered one simple sentence.

"Stay here. Let me handle this."

She walked over to the phone and picked up the receiver, static crackling over the line as the call connected. Based on what Trish has told me since, the conversation probably went a little like this:

"Hello, is Trish Mardero there?"

"This is she Larry ... and I'm told we have some important things to discuss."

"Err, yes," Mr. Grassini stumbled slightly before regaining composure. "So Adam told you what happened today?"

"He did," Trish replied, pursing her lips. "And I have to admit, I'm not very impressed."

"Neither was I to be honest — Adam is one of our better students. I never would have expected this from him."

"That's not what I meant ..." Trish quipped, the 'and you know it' being heavily implied.

"Excuse me?"

"Larry, you aren't suspending Adam."

"But Mrs. Mardero ... Trish ... you know as well as I do the board has a zero-tolerance policy, and Adam broke it." Mr. Grassini implored.

"Larry, listen to me, Adam has been bullied for the better part of two years at your school, and no one has done anything about it. I can't blame him for finally having enough and standing up to those jerks. It's them you should be going after, not my son."

"Mrs. Mardero, I wish it was that simple, but —"

"Oh it *is* that simple, Larry. You see, I'm at the board office tomorrow, and meeting with Chuck. You know Chuck, right?"

"Yes ... I am acquainted with the director of education ..."

"Good. Chuck and I go way back. We have lunch most weeks together, and just yesterday he was telling me how impressed he was by the work you and your VP have done at St. Francis. It would be a *real shame* if I happened to mention any of this to him tomorrow, wouldn't it?"

"I understand," Mr. Grassini replied quietly. "Adam will of course not be suspended. I have to give him an in-school suspension though: half a day, tomorrow afternoon."

"Great. I knew you'd understand, Larry. Thank you."

With that, Trish hung up the phone, and looked over at me, smirking.

"Heard all of that, did you?"

"Most of it, yeah."

"Good," Trish nodded. "Now you know Adam, violence is never the solution, right? Larry ... er ... Mr. Grassini was only following the rules the board tells us all to follow."

"I know, mum," I replied, bowing my head.

"Alright then," her tone became almost conspiratorial.

"Then between you and me? Those jerks had that coming!"

§

There were other times I didn't get so lucky. Take the time I wrote an epic science fiction ballad for a poetry assignment, and after proudly presenting it to the class, one of my classmates snidely told me to "go back to *Deep Space Nine*" (which I would have loved to do if only Starfleet would send a damned rescue ship to save me). All that said: the whole class laughed. My self esteem fractured a little more as I sank back into my seat.

Sad. Angry. Alone. When I think back on it all, this is still how I feel. It's not the kind of thing you can just get over. Middle school was the worst time of my life. I might have endured a depressive episode in the aftermath of my parents' divorce, but this was something else. It felt like I had a target painted on my back the moment I started at St. Francis, and try as I might, I couldn't get it off. The bullies had found their mark, and it was me.

I've heard it said in autistic and neurodiversity advocacy circles that kids will never admit to or even consciously be aware of the fact that they're bullying someone for being autistic. Typically, when called on their behaviour, most bullies will deny that as their motivation, and instead mention how their target was awkward, obsessed with strange things, quiet, or otherwise 'weird.' The thing is, all of these traits are strongly associated with autism, and so whether they realize it or not, bullies tend to pick on fellow kids who are autistic to a high degree. Speaking from personal experience, this rings true to me.

Looking back, it's possible ... even probable ... that Ritchie and Geo were lashing out because of their own issues. Who knows? Maybe they had complicated home lives they were processing in the only way they knew how. Perhaps they'd only ever known toxic male role models and so had never been taught how to be kind young men. Then again, maybe they really were just mean. It made little difference to me at the time, and there's not really any excuse for treating other people like that.

During those years, I routinely felt suicidal thoughts pass through my mind. They were never severe enough that I would have acted on them, but they were there all the same. I was just so filled with anger, despair, and loneliness that I honestly couldn't believe it would ever get better, despite every adult telling me otherwise.

What stopped my thoughts of suicide from becoming anything more than just thoughts? Love. The one thing I never stopped believing during those dark years was that there were those in my life who loved and valued me unconditionally. People like Trish, my dad, my mom, and Mitch, who always leant a sympathetic ear and were there when I needed them most. Mitch and I saw each other almost every night after school, and though I didn't see a lot of Saria and Drew because of how big St. Francis was, it made a difference knowing they were around too. They also had their issues with Geo and Ritchie. Even Brian had found his way to St. Francis, and I gravitated toward him and some other nerdy kids I met. It's thanks to them I was able to pull through and move past these thoughts. When I say I believe in the power of love and optimism, it isn't just idealism; these things literally saved my life.

CHAPTER 10

Middle school was without a doubt the worst time in my life, but it wasn't all bad. Take my first experience with Autism advocacy, for example. I'm referring to one moment in Grade 7 that still stands out: the speech writing competition.

I've always been a creative person, but I discovered my love of writing in a somewhat funny and unexpected way. As a kid, I always saw myself as more of a visual artist. I loved drawing and cartooning and was on track to become fairly decent at it. The problem was I often found myself drawing and doodling in class instead of paying attention to what the teacher was saying. I have always had difficulty maintaining interest in things that don't appeal to me — which is a typical trait for people with both autism and ADHD. So, in their well-meaning way, after the third note from my teacher in as many weeks, my parents told me I was no longer allowed to draw in class; I had to pay attention.

Without realizing it, with this, my parents actually granted me one of the best gifts they ever could have. Being decidedly stubborn — and unwilling to endure the mind-numbing boredom of paying attention to lessons I wasn't interested in to begin with — my parents' ban on visual art during class just forced me to become more underhanded and sneaky in performing my rebellious acts of creativity under the teacher's nose.

If I couldn't draw in class, I would start writing instead.

After only a few months, writing had become far more to me than just a creative way to circumvent the rules. I started really imagining and inventing worlds for myself, brought to life not by drawings, but by words on a page. More than that, I actually found the ability to go far deeper into my own imagination through the written word than I'd ever been able to do through visual art. One of the first projects I ever tackled was finally telling the story of the imaginative games Drew, Saria, and I had played during recess in elementary school all those years ago; a strange mix of the *Pokémon* and *Legend of Zelda* video game franchises that we'd affectionately taken to calling "Zeldamon." It sounds silly in retrospect, but at the time, it really helped me find my way as a writer. Words just seemed to have magic to them, and I often wondered how I hadn't discovered the liberating joy of writing sooner.

Imagine my delight when an opportunity to put my newfound skill and passion to work presented itself: there was going to be a speech writing competition. The rules were simple: each Grade 7 student at St. Francis was required to write a speech and present it in front of their class. The topic could be anything that interested us. The class would vote on the best speeches and the winners would earn a gift certificate to a bookstore of their choosing, and of course, the respect of their peers.

It was a shameless popularity contest. But it also excited me.

Deciding what to write about wasn't easy, though I did have an idea. A seemingly absurd and dangerous one. It was embarrassing and terrifying even to think about doing it.

And yet, it also carried with it some allure.

Both Starfleet officers and Jedi Knights are trained to stand up to injustice and embrace their personal truths. They differ in how they go about this, but at the core they share the same values. These were the media role models that spoke to me at the time, so I decided that this would be my own personal opportunity to both know myself better, and to stand up for myself in a peaceful way befitting both the Jedi and Starfleet codes.

I decided to write my speech about Asperger's Syndrome. Why I thought it was a good idea to write about this when I was already a target for bullying is beyond me. Being autistic wasn't something I was open about at the time (in fact, I felt extremely defensive about even the thought of it being true), and it was only as I grew older that I began to really understand what the diagnosis meant for me. Partly, I think even though I had a complicated relationship with the word Asperger's, on some level I really did want to know more about it. I'm inquisitive by nature after all. Maybe it would help me understand why Dr. Jackson had diagnosed me with it to begin with. Partly — idealistically perhaps — I also think I hoped by writing about myself and how I was different, my classmates would understand me and bully me less. If nothing else, it was a nice dream. One thing is clear: I was either very brave, or very reckless. I think it may have been a bit of both.

Armed with purpose, I set out to educate myself and my classmates. It was high time I learned more for myself anyway, and as I cracked open the book my dad had given me (a delightfully geared-to-children read called "Asperger's Huh?" that followed the adventures of a boy with Asperger's), I immediately saw myself in the main character. It all checked out; an obsessive interest in the things he loved (in his case, the weather, in my own, video games, science fiction, and technology), awkward interactions with his peers, all of it. Parts of it didn't sit well with me (I didn't appreciate the author's recommendation to just "not tell jokes" as humour was something I held dear, even if I didn't always get it right), but overall, it was fascinating. For the first time ever, I felt I knew exactly what Asperger's was, and why Dr. Jackson had seen fit to diagnose me with it.

The speech rapidly became an obsession for me, and for the next several weeks, I lived and breathed Asperger's, talking and thinking about nothing else as I hammered away at my project. I think it's safe to say that I annoyed anyone and everyone I could manage to start a conversation with — I was that into it. My sleepover with Brian at my mom's house one weekend? Ironically consumed by talk of Asperger's and how it often led me to being single-minded about my interests. My dad and Trish? Asperger's, how it was seen by the professionals of the day as one of many points on the autistic spectrum, and why they got me checked out by Dr. Jackson. Mitch and other friends? That's right; a heaping dose of yet more Aspergianisms. I rambled about everything from echolalia and stimming (which are repetitive sounds and movements that feel oh so good) to how difficult I sometimes found social interactions to anyone who would listen. Ironically, autism dominated my thoughts in the most autistic way imaginable. I may not have been open about being "on the spectrum" (a term I came to learn as I was writing), but I was certainly excited to learn everything there was to know about it. In retrospect, so much of the language used was clinical and mistakenly treated autism/Asperger's as though it was a defect (because even when books of the time tried to be supportive, they inevitably oozed with ableism and tragedy). Despite this, I was relieved to finally have some understanding of why I was the way I was.

Maybe I do have Asperger's after all, I mused. And maybe, that's okay.

When the day finally came to present our speeches, I was so nervous I could feel my stomach turning and drops of sweat crawling down my skin. All morning, the tension built until I was stretched so thin I could barely handle it, but finally it was time for the speeches. After several of my classmates had gotten up and delivered their speeches on the usual topics (friends, family, sports), my turn came at last. Clutching my notes in my sweaty hands, I got up and began the long march to the front of the class. As I gazed around the room and saw my classmates staring expectantly back at me, my anxiety instantly spiked, then miraculously began to dissipate.

Without waiting to see if it would come back, I launched into my speech. "Teachers, classmates, judges, and fellow contestants," I began. "Today I want to talk to you all about a little something called Asperger's."

From that moment on, I took a deep breath and got right into it, stopping only to occasionally breathe. I covered everything from the history of the condition to the symptoms, and my own experiences growing up with it. I explained to my classmates in no uncertain terms that it was responsible for everything from my intense passion for all things sci-fi to my social awkwardness and difficulty regulating my emotions. At first, my chest was tight, and my heart skipped a beat as I spoke so openly and vulnerably, but as my speech progressed, I felt less and less apprehensive around the Asperger's label. In fact, I even began to feel a little pride. I was me, and now, everyone was going to know it.

When I finished, the class went silent for what felt like an eternity, giving my anxiety the opportunity to flood my brain as I processed the aftermath. *Oh no,* I thought to myself, rapidly spiralling into an anxiety whirlpool. *No, no, no. I shouldn't have done that. They hated it, and now I gave them more ammo than ever to bully me.*

Not long after I uttered the last word of my speech, though, the class burst into thunderous applause. I had impressed them after all. They loved it! I exhaled sharply, feeling the tension drain out and be replaced with excitement for their praise.

I won't lie, this went to my head. I had advocated for myself, and based on their reaction, I figured I had the contest in the bag. *How could anyone else win?* I wondered to myself. *I clearly had the most original speech. I clearly went above and beyond. I'm bound to win.*

Unfortunately, as I've said many times by now, I didn't like to lose, nor did I know how to do so gracefully, though I was about to learn. My speech didn't even make the final running — it was ousted by some account of what it takes to win at hockey by one of the class jocks. I was gutted; after all that effort, all that vulnerability, and all that self-exploration, I didn't even get an honourable mention!

It stung, and I felt extremely demoralized and humiliated.

A funny thing happened though; by the end of the day, several of my classmates had come up to me and started asking me questions about Asperger's. Even Ritchie, my incessant bully and middle school nemesis, came up and asked about things I'd talked about. I was terrified to answer, but did so truthfully all the same (What the hell? The damage had already been done). Ultimately, some small part of me was inspired by the fact that even if my classmates hadn't chosen my speech to win, it had at least made some of them think.

Did self-advocacy end the bullying and make my life better in middle school? Not in the slightest. Only moving on to high school would start to change things. Still, it was good to reclaim the word Asperger's for myself a bit that day. I felt emboldened as I admitted to myself and others that this was who I was. That day in 2001, I embraced myself as autistic for the first time. It was the moment where the philosophy of self-acceptance I hold today began to form, even if it took far longer for it to cement itself in my brain. Self-acceptance is often an up-and-down path, and my life was no exception to that.

In *The Dark Knight* — the second instalment of Chris Nolan's *Dark Knight* trilogy — Harvey Dent says the night is always darkest just before the dawn, and that the dawn is coming. So too would it be with my own life — after just a little more darkness, that is.

Chapter 11

"What do you mean you need to move?"

I sat trembling on my bed, clutching the phone to my ear as I listened to my mother explain how both of our lives were going to change drastically. I was about to graduate from St. Francis, and while I was scared of the bullying following me into high school, I had also become cautiously optimistic about a fresh start. My mom's announcement was the last thing I expected to hear. There was silence on the line, only the static of our terrible, early-2000s VOIP phone connection breaking up as my mom composed herself.

"I need to move to Kingston to be closer to the help I need Adam," she said. "My therapist stopped offering it, and no one else here does — believe me, I've looked. Besides, Grandma is getting older, and I want to make sure she's okay."

"But what about me?" I asked desperately, feeling the tears well up in my eyes. "I don't want you to go."

"I know sweetie," my mom sighed. If I had listened closely, I would have heard her voice trembling and understood she took no joy at the prospect of moving away from her son. At the time, I was more self-absorbed.

"But just think," she began, trying to console me, "you'll still be able to call me whenever you want, and you can come visit me for a whole month in the summer."

"It's not the same," I shot back. "I don't just want to see

you for a month, I want to see you all the time, like we do right now."

"I know honey, and I'm sorry," my mother replied quietly. "If there was another way, I'd do it. But I can't get better if I stay here."

"I know ...," I said. The reality of the situation was starting to sink in.

"You'll be able to visit for a whole month," my mom repeated, taking advantage of my calmer state to try and sell me a bit more on the idea. "You can visit your uncle and aunt and cousin and Grandma. They have a pool ... remember how much fun you had when we visited them last time?"

It was true; I had really enjoyed myself when we visited three years earlier. Immediately, I found myself imagining swimming and barbecues and ...

"I guess it could be fun ..."

"It will be."

It sounded as though my mom was trying to convince herself as much as me, and for the moment it had worked. As sad as I was that she was moving, I officially had yet another reason to look forward to the end of the year (as if I needed one); I was going to Kingston.

Maybe my Starfleet rescue ship was on its way after all.

§

Trish and my dad have always looked out for me — and been damn good parents overall — but any time I needed emotional, social, or philosophical advice, my mom was always a phone call or a visit away. It was hard to accept that, after two of the darkest years of my life, one of my biggest supporters was leaving town.

By that point, my mom had been getting treatment for her mental health struggles for years in Sudbury and was generally in a good place. However, in 2002, as I was getting ready to graduate, the specific therapies she required stopped being offered locally. She had no choice but to seek them out elsewhere and she settled on Kingston, a seven-hour drive to the southeast. The rest of Ontario has always had more funding for medical services than the north where we lived, and there was the added benefit that her mother lived there, along with her brother, sister-in-law, and nephew. The family could be closer together.

Once I had gotten past my initial emotional outburst, I had to admit certain parts of the plan appealed. In particular, my mother told me she planned to have me down visiting her for half of my summer break. The plan was that I would attend my graduation ceremony, then after a celebratory dinner with the whole family at East Side Mario's, I would skip town and head south. Missing the grad dance didn't bother me in the slightest. After how awful those two years were, I had no love lost toward many of my classmates, and no qualms moving on with my life. The night after school ended, I found myself jumping for joy down the front steps of that accursed building, jubilant and triumphant. It was over; I had survived.

§

The day after our family dinner at East Sides', I was off to the airport for my flight to Kingston; a medium-sized city on the coast of Lake Ontario that once served as the pre-Confederation capital of Ontario back when it was known as Upper Canada. The city was chock full of history, and I was excited by what felt like a whole new world to explore.

I still wasn't sure how I felt about my mom moving away. It really did feel like I'd come to a safe place though — a port in the storm after my middle school experience. As I disembarked from my flight in the Kingston airport, I smiled as I saw my mom standing there waiting for me, along with an older woman sporting greying blond hair — my Grandma Agnes.

"Hi sweetie." My mom seemed to light up as I ran over and gave her the biggest hug.

"How was your flight, darling?" That was my grandma. She seemed very happy to see me too.

"Scary at first," I replied honestly. I had been terrified to get on my flight alone. "It was okay once I got used to it though."

"Good I'm glad. I was worried sick about you." My mom pulled me in closer.

"Want to get out of here and go somewhere to eat?"

Food? After the stressful day I'd had? My mouth grew into the biggest smile.

"Sure!"

§

As it turned out, my Grandma Agnes and my mom lived in two apartment buildings that were part of the same complex, situated opposite each other. That night, after driving us in from the airport, my mom offered to bring her out for dinner with us as a thank you for the ride. She accepted happily, and we made for the Rose and Crown — a family eatery and Irish pub located in the nearby Cataraqui Town Centre mall. It was brightly lit, with Irish paraphernalia hanging from the green walls and stylized wooden dividers separating the booths. We sat in one close to the door so that my mom could have easy access to a smoke break throughout the meal if need be. I immediately loved the atmosphere.

"So sweetie, how does it feel to have taken the plane alone for the first time?" Mom asked. I shrugged. I was exhausted, slightly rattled, and yet also happy to have arrived. All of this came out in my speech.

"Kinda weird? It's strange to be so far from everyone, but it also feels really good to see you mom."

"I can understand that honey," she replied. "This is a huge step out of your comfort zone, and it's natural to feel a little scared."

She doesn't know the half of it, I thought to myself as I looked back at her. At that point, my Grandma Agnes joined the conversation.

"I'm *so* happy you're here, darling," she exclaimed, a warm smile spreading over her face as she spoke. She reached a hand out for mine and gripped it hard. "It's been so long since I've seen you. You'll have to come over for grilled cheese sandwiches, just like I used to make for you when I lived in Sudbury. Mhmm."

My grandma's words made me feel warm and fuzzy inside. It was true — we hadn't seen each other in years. She used to live in Sudbury but opted to move to Kingston in the mid-90s. In her own words, "there was more to do there." Part of me was excited to find out if that was in fact true.

"You can't have him *all* the time, mum," my mom chastised playfully. "After all, I want to see my son a bit too, and between you and his aunt and uncle, I'm going to have him torn three ways from Sunday."

"Oh, Lynne come on now," Agnes admonished. "I'm just excited to see my grandson is all. So where are they by the way. Judy's been asking me when they get to see him."

"I know, I talked to Percy the other day. He mentioned they'd made up the guest bedroom for whenever Adam wanted to go over and stay the night." My mom sighed. "It's good to have the family together, but I'd at least like one night with my son before the rest of you get your grubby paws on him."

I laughed at the banter. It was hard to describe exactly, but I immediately had a sense of comfort and familiarity. It was as though I was meant to be there.

"Can I go see Uncle Percy and Aunt Judy this week, mom?" I asked. She looked at me and smiled.

"Of course, honey. I'll call them tonight when we get home and make the arrangements. But first; where's our server? I'm starved."

At that, I grinned in spite of myself. Some things never changed, and throughout the years, mom's presence feeling like home was one of them.

My visit was already off to a pretty great start.

§

Visiting Kingston that summer was a life-changing experience. I finally got a chance to know my extended family a little better, and my cousin Jack and I hit it off quickly, becoming fast friends. He and I spent hours and hours just talking about science fiction and video games and building spaceships out of LEGO. We also spent an equal amount of time playing out epic space battles and crafting narratives around our creations. In him, I found a kindred spirit of a sort I hadn't commonly found back home, and our family certainly began to see many similarities between us. Mitch and I were the best of friends sure, but Jack was another person who just seemed to *get* me.

I ended up having a similarly instant connection with my aunt and uncle too. In fact, I first realized they were a different kind of people when I saw the massive wood bookshelf my Aunt Judy claimed as her own; a huge collection of *Star Wars* Expanded Universe novels, *Star Trek* books, and other science fiction classics like Frank Herbert's *Dune*. They even had my favourite *Star Wars* saga — the *Thrawn Trilogy*, by Timothy Zhan. When I asked about her collection, she grinned and launched enthusiastically into an explanation. Soon we were joined by both my uncle and cousin, who were themselves just as enthusiastic, and before I knew it ... hours had passed. I'd rarely met anyone else who shared my level of interest and excitement about all things nerdy, let alone three at once! At home, I often felt like the only one; the proverbial wizard, living in muggle land. But with my aunt, uncle, and cousin? I felt understood in a way I never had before.

It was true; Starfleet had finally come. My rescue ship had arrived at last.

§

Of course, I soon learned some interesting facts about the crew of the rescue ship. My Grandma Agnes, for example, loved numbers, could talk for hours about politics or economics, and wouldn't catch a joke being made in conversation even if it was being drawn in the air by a Boeing 747 flying low overhead (which quickly became a family in-joke). My Uncle Percy could easily design an entire modular back deck and build it himself despite being completely self-taught (and in fact, he had). My cousin Jack for his part had his own social struggles just like I did, but he was also a wizard with computers and technology. Even my Aunt Judy had her own nerdy eccentricities — she collected books and dragon statues — along with the kind of interesting past that always made for great stories.

In short, they were my people. It didn't surprise me at all to later learn that they were all either autistic or otherwise neurologically unique.

Because we shared similar brain wiring, my extended family taught me some good survival techniques for life on the autistic spectrum. This went a long way toward helping me become more comfortable with my own Asperger's diagnosis, even if I wasn't ready to admit it at the time. After everything I'd been through in middle school, acknowledging this fact about myself wasn't something I really wanted to do, and yet being around them — seeing them normalize autistic life for me — began to change my mindset on a deeper level. I still didn't like when they'd mention it — it always felt as though they were bringing up something that was *wrong* with me — but they never acted like that, and in fact often had good advice.

One of the most important early lessons my Aunt Judy taught me is one she referred to as "the three strikes of telling a joke." A few days into my visit with her, I was joking around — using the same joke I'd told upward of half a dozen times by that point — while everyone around me struggled to tolerate the repetition. After one too many times, my aunt rolled her eyes and sighed, deciding to intervene.

"The first time you tell someone a joke, if it's funny they'll laugh a lot," she explained. "The second time, it'll be less funny, and the third time and on it just won't be funny at all."

That might sound like common sense, but for someone on the autistic spectrum, this wasn't immediately obvious. I always assumed that because I enjoyed hearing my jokes over and over, others would too. In a weird way, I even took some pleasure in the groans I elicited. *Surely, they were having as much fun as I was, right?*

Spoiler alert: they were not.

By providing me with a framework, my aunt and uncle helped me understand why such a rule might exist. Having such a grounding gave my analytical brain what it needed to know itself better, and I definitely grew from the lesson.

§

"But I don't want to go home. Why can't you come with me?" I looked deep into my mom's eyes and gave her the biggest hug as tears began rolling down my cheeks. The summer had flown by faster than I'd expected, and we'd finally reached the part I dreaded most, saying goodbye. Intellectually, I understood why my mom had to move — she couldn't get what she needed back home — but that was cold comfort and didn't make things any easier. I suddenly understood exactly how Wesley Crusher must have felt when he left his mother Dr. Beverly Crusher to attend Starfleet Academy. In fact, that's exactly how my brain processed it. Just as Wesley would go on to miss Captain Picard, Data, Riker, Troi, and his mom, so too would I miss my family and long for any opportunity to see them again.

"I know, honey, but I'll only be a phone call away."

"It won't be the same," I argued, repeating something I'd been saying ever since she first broke the news to me. It wouldn't be the same. Other kids had their parents around — Mitch got to see his mom whenever he wanted — why couldn't I?

"I know ..." My mom sighed and pulled me close, stroking my hair as we held each other for what felt like hours.

"Remember what I said on the beach on Manitoulin years ago? I'm not going anywhere sweetie. I promise. Distance can't keep us apart."

"You promise?" She nodded.

"I promise. I love you, Adam."

"I love you too, mom."

Letting go of my mom and turning to board the plane back

to Sudbury was one of the hardest things I'd ever done. It broke my heart to leave her behind, and I bawled for days after the fact. But mom was right — she didn't go anywhere, and neither did my uncle, aunt, cousin, and grandma. It was hard at first, but she and I talked every week on the phone, and I went back to visit several times per year.

I may not have been ready to fully accept my place on the spectrum yet, nor was I particularly happy to have left my mom in Kingston just as I was starting Grade 9 at a new school in September, but I also knew I wasn't alone anymore.

I was being sent back on another long-term assignment on an alien world, but Starfleet was no longer out of contact — in fact, they were more in contact now than ever. And it was support that I desperately needed as I faced the next chapter of my life.

CHAPTER 12

There I was, alone in a sea of blue and green uniformed bodies, packed like sardines into the cavernous entrance hall of my new school. It was my first day of high school, and nothing could have prepared me for how it felt. After two rough years in middle school, I was nervous the same kids who made my life miserable there would follow me to high school and continue their reign of torment. This never happened, but high school was not without its own challenges — one of the biggest being the sheer size of the thing. Simply put, St. Benedict Catholic Secondary School felt huge. At the time, it had roughly 500 students, and while that may not sound particularly big, for an autistic person from a smaller Northern Ontario city? This couldn't have been more intimidating. Crowds have always made me feel anxious and overwhelmed, and that first day of Grade 9, I was surrounded by more people than I'd ever seen before. Naturally, my anxiety spiked. Nevertheless, I kept my head held high and plowed through the masses, eventually finding some familiar faces.

"Saria," I called out. My grade school friend was sitting by herself near the cafeteria doors. She turned and looked at me, smiling.

"Hey Adam," she said, apparently as happy as I was to find a friend in this horde. "This is wild, isn't it?"

"Oh my gosh, I know," I replied. "It's a bit exhausting to be honest."

"It really is," she agreed. "I thought St. Francis was big. Oh well, hopefully we won't have to deal with Geo and Ritchie ..."

The sight of Ritchie walking by did nothing to ease our discomfort.

"Well, there's jerk-face number one," I quipped, ignoring the dread in the pit of my stomach. "I wonder where jerk-face number two is ..."

"No need to worry about him," Saria said, smiling. "Apparently Geo switched schools, he's going to Lo-Ellen this year."

Immediately, my heart grew lighter. Lo-Ellen was all the way on the other side of town; in high school distance, a world away. Even if Ritchie was at St. Bens, I couldn't help but feel that, given how big this place was, and that he was lacking his partner in crime, there wasn't much he could do to torment us.

"That's awesome," I enthused. Saria nodded as the bell chimed.

"I know I'm glad too. If I had to put up with him calling me "fish lips" one more time ..." She cringed at the thought of it, and so did I.

We chuckled and followed the crowd toward the classrooms. Much like the beginning of a *Harry Potter* novel, we were ushered off to our assigned home rooms where we'd learn the ropes of the new school.

While the large student population terrified me at first, I soon learned it was one of my greatest advantages. Despite my initial feeling of being lost and adrift, going to a bigger school allowed me to find my own way. It didn't hurt, of course, that we were all feeling similarly. At last, I could be my own person, and not worry about past baggage. It was a fresh start after all.

§

Of course, even though I'd started enjoying the new beginning high school allowed, I was still scared of others learning about things like my obsessive love of video games, science fiction, and technology in general, or worse — the fact I had Asperger's. I shuddered as I thought about the previous two years and forced myself to push the worries out of my mind.

No need to think about any of that anymore, I negotiated with myself. You're here now. It's over.

I was sitting in the cafeteria on my first day of school, picking at my lunch. It was a panzerotti from the school servery — essentially a giant pizza pocket slathered in tomato sauce and filled with cheese, pepperoni, and yet more tomato sauce. It was also easily the most popular item on the menu at St. Bens. That day in particular, I needed such comfort food because pushing anxiety out of your brain never works for long. I was afraid no one would talk to me, and equally afraid that the wrong people would. My social awkwardness and passionate interests had only ever brought me pain and sadness in the past ... at least in a public setting. No, it was best to eat lunch alone and read my copy of Nintendo Power in peace.

"Is anyone sitting here?"

I looked up nervously, feeling apprehensive as I laid eyes on the source of the voice. He was scrawny with long blond hair obscuring his face. He looked kind of like Cousin It from The Addams Family. I slid my tray over the open magazine and replied, my eyes alternating between uncomfortable contact and looking awkwardly back down at the table.

"Oh, um ... no," my voice quiet. "You ... you can sit here if you want?"

"Sure," he replied and sat down before I even realized what was going on. "I'm Chris, by the way."

"Adam," I answered. He did seem friendly and approachable, so I started to let my guard down and went back to reading my magazine.

"Is that an issue of Nintendo Power?" He asked. I froze. Of course, he would notice, I thought to myself. Of course, he'd call me on it.

Being autistic in situations like these often feels like playing a video game and being presented with dialog options when you interact with another character. You're never sure exactly which one to pick, or what the most desired option is before you do, so you kind of need to just click on one and hope for the best. Of course, before I even had a chance to flip through my choices in that initial conversation with Chris (possibilities included "Oh it's not mine (Bluff: 20)" and "What's a Nintendo Power? (Deception: 40)"), I noticed he looked genuinely interested. Enthusiastically so, in fact — he'd taken the issue and pulled it over to where he sat, using one hand to wipe the long hair out of his eyes as he flipped through the pages with the other. I recognized his intensity as what I too felt when discussing video games.

I grinned. I wasn't even mad he'd lost my page.

"Do you ... like video games too?" I asked. He looked up, his eyes wide.

"Do I like video games? I don't think "like" is a strong enough word."

I smiled and relaxed, overjoyed to have found someone with whom I had things in common. It was something I'd only ever really experienced with Mitch and my elementary school friends, and it had been years since I'd had something like that happen at school.

"Oh this is the new issue isn't it?" Chris asked. He sounded ecstatic. "All about Metroid Prime?"

"It is! I really can't wait for it to come out. I've never played any of the old Metroid games, but I just got a GameCube last year, and that game looks awesome."

"You're so lucky you have a Cube man," Chris replied. His jaw then dropped as he registered the second part of what I'd just said.

"Wait ... did you just say you've never played any of the old Metroid games?"

"Well, I mean I found the old NES one at a second-hand store when I went with my mom in grade school but ..."

"But like ... you've never played Super Metroid?" I shook my head, and Chris gasped.

"Well then you need to. I might even have the ROM for my Super Nintendo emulator at home that I could give you ..."

"What's an emulator?" I was genuinely curious. Chris's jaw dropped even further.

"You know? A computer program that lets you play old games on your PC?"

"You can do that?" It was my turn to be shocked. My jaw dropped as well, and Chris smiled.

"It's a good thing I came along when I did, isn't it?" He laughed, then looked at me dead on from across the table, feigning seriousness as his voice went deep.

"Now Adam, are you ready to see just how far down the video game rabbit hole goes?"

I chuckled at his obvious reference to The Matrix and nodded, heart pounding in excitement and thoroughly absorbed in the conversation. This went on all lunch. As we walked out of the cafeteria a half hour later, we continued our conversation until we parted ways and went to our respective classes. Befriending Chris made me feel less alone. Finding someone who shared my interests with almost the same level of intensity went a long way toward helping to rebuild the self-esteem that had been so thoroughly trounced in middle school. I couldn't stop grinning.

Maybe this high school thing isn't going to be so bad after all.

§

Chris and I continued to hang out at lunch, and eventually others joined us at our little aisle table in the middle of the St. Bens cafeteria. It felt like the beginning of a brand-new adventuring party; almost as though this was to be the higher budget modern sequel to the old-school RPG (Role-Playing Game) that was my time at St. Theresa. Of course, as befit any modernization of a classic video game, new game mechanics were introduced, and as an autistic person I definitely struggled to learn some of them — especially the newly expanded social interaction system. Despite the fact Chris and I really seemed to understand each other (which isn't surprising considering he's since told me he has ADHD), I found myself dealing with a new facet of it every day at lunch.

"Hey Adam, want a cookie?"

My head perked up immediately from my Game Boy Advance. I was playing some lunch-hour *Super Mario* in the cafeteria. Like a puppy, I glanced over at Tim (one of the new people who had found his way over to us), practically drooling. He held a massive, perfectly browned peanut butter cookie in his hands. From the look on his face, I should have realized that something was not quite right, but my autistic brain didn't clue in.

"Why don't you want it?" I asked, looking suspiciously from the cookie back to Tim. He shrugged as he replied.

"I'm not hungry anymore. Don't want it to go to waste. So ... do you want it?"

At that point, having decided his admittedly bare-bones story checked out (because yay, autistic social naivety), I nodded enthusiastically.

With all the rabidness of a food-starved Pavlovian dog, I reached for the cookie and took a huge bite. My head swam. I love peanut butter cookies, and that particular one had sent me to a peanutty paradise ... until I looked up at Tim, sitting across the table. He was giggling as our eyes met, and the look on his face was one of triumph.

"What?" I mumbled through the remaining cookie, perplexed at his reaction. He stopped giggling for a second.

"I licked that cookie."

My heart and my mind raced. *He LICKED it?* I knew Tim was a trickster, so I wasn't entirely sure what to believe. Was his prank licking the cookie and feeding it to me? Or was it in making me *believe* he had? For my neurodivergent brain, deciphering which option it was felt like rolling a D20 (twenty-sided dice) for a Perception check in a game of *Dungeons and Dragons*, only to not be given a definitive answer either way. And if you'll excuse the pun, it drove me nuts.

"Did you really?" I managed at last. "Because I don't think you did."

"How do you know?" Tim shot back, intent on continuing the game.

"Because you can't have," I replied, attempting to apply logic to the situation. "I didn't see any wet spots on the cookie."

"Okay," answered Tim cryptically.

"So, you didn't?" I asked, hopeful.

"What do you think?" He answered, delighting in playing on my gullibility. He smiled and walked away as the bell rang signifying the end of lunch.

It was as though the metaphorical D20 had defied physics and landed on one of its points, rendering my Perception check utterly moot. Needless to say, this occupied my frantic thoughts for the rest of the day.

§

Another aspect of the new social interaction system I struggled with as an autistic person in the RPG of high school was knowing when my friends were engaging in good natured teasing vs when I was being bullied. The difference was really subtle, and I never was very good at it. This perplexing situation was at the forefront of my mind as I sat with my friends one morning, trying to enjoy some quiet time before class.

"Oh look, Merdy's got his nose buried in a book again," Brian teased as he arrived and sat down. He was probably grinning or wearing a playful look on his face, but I was too absorbed in what I was reading to notice.

I cringed, arm hairs standing on end as I looked up from my book — a copy of *Star Wars X-Wing: Rogue Squadron* by Michael A. Stackpole that I'd picked up at Chapters during a recent visit. Merdy was a nickname granted me by Tim — a condensed version of my last name Mardero — that the entirety of my high school friend group embraced before long. None of us — Tim included — had any idea at the time that in French, *merde* meant shit; my friends simply thought it was a playful term of endearment and a clever shortening of my surname. I'd never been given a nickname before, and getting one felt as though I'd been officially accepted into the group. It made me smile in spite of myself. Because of that, I let them have it, and even embraced it.

"I ... I am not!"

"Really?" Brian smirked as he pointed at the well-worn paperback sitting on top of my zip-up binder. "What do you call that then?"

"I ... just like *Star Wars*, okay?"

I often had a hard time responding to situations like this as an autistic person. It felt like I was being asked to roll yet another Perception check, only this time with a D20 that had a mind of its own. Was Brian just ribbing me as a friend? I was never quite sure.

"Merdy's our book nerd, man," interjected Chris. "He's been reading since the day we met."

I laughed, still feeling somewhat uncomfortable about Brian's teasing, but processing the situation a bit. As I did though, Brian reached over and grabbed my book from its resting place on top of my stack of class binders. This infuriated me, though I tried not to let my anger betray itself.

"Hey. That's not funny, give it back!" He started reading a passage out loud. It drove me bonkers and made my skin crawl when people did that; I scowled.

"Sorry man," Brian teased, "I was just wondering if I'd like this book too."

Had I passed my Charisma check in that moment, I might have said something along the lines of "If you're so curious, buy your own." Sadly, I've never been that quick-witted. I was like a deer caught in the headlights, and it didn't help that Brian was using sarcasm—something I hadn't fully mastered either. It was a double whammy of awfulness.

"Really?" I queried apprehensively at last. Brian shrugged. "I mean, maybe," he replied, having realized I really wasn't sure. He smiled and handed the book back to me. "I was just kidding around though man; you're awesome."

"Yeah, I figured," I lied. I hadn't figured, but I felt super awkward and uncomfortable. I didn't want to admit I didn't know he was joking. I also didn't want to admit the whole thing had hurt me. After all, friends teased each other, right?

There is a *very* fine line between friendly teasing and its cruel cousin taunting. Sometimes, even friends accidentally crossed this line without realizing it, so my confusion was valid. As the bell rang and we all got up to go to class though, it occurred to me perhaps an essential clue to the teasing vs bullying mystery lay in the backgrounds of the people doing it. The character backstories if you will. I decided then and there that if someone was my friend and had proven it many times in the past, there was a greater chance that they were kidding around. It wasn't a foolproof system, but it was a start and having a structure to follow helped my autistic brain parse out some of these complicated social situations a bit better. It also lead me to critically re-evaluate some of the people who claimed to be my friends. I smiled, knowing I'd never again have to eat a licked cookie.

I just had received +1 to all future perception checks.

CHAPTER 13

How DARE they?
I was incensed. Indignant. Offended beyond belief. How dare they think I needed any sort of accommodation at all? I was okay dammit. I was normal. I was *fine*.
It all began one morning in January of Grade 9. St. Benedict Catholic Secondary School was rapidly approaching exam time, and as we did, the stress level in the school was palpable. It was like a thick, unpleasant, steamy mist filling the halls as we studied, crammed, and just plain panicked our way to the final assessments of our fall semester.
At least, that was how I felt. I couldn't really be sure about anyone else, but I was *very* nervous that first exam month ... a fact that wasn't helped by Trish and my dad, who saw fit to give me an *extremely* rigid and structured exam study schedule with little to no room for breaks. It went something like this:
3:00pm-3:30pm: Get home from School
3:30pm-4:30pm: Study Geography
4:30pm-5:30pm: Dinner
5:30pm-6:30pm: Study English
6:30pm-6:45pm: Break
6:45pm-7:45pm: Study Math
7:45pm-8:45pm: Study Computers
8:45pm-9:15pm: Quick Review
9:15pm-10pm: Free time before bed

To say I found this overwhelming and exhausting would be putting it mildly. But I pushed on, fighting past my executive dysfunction as best I could. I found that while I needed structure like this in order to work well, I also felt suffocated by the rigidity of it — as though there was a tug-of-war going on in my brain over what worked best for it. Nevertheless, I studied, prepared myself, and genuinely began to feel ready for my first exam (Math, with the bald and intimidating Mr. Iroh) when *it* happened.

I was leaving home room one morning to go to my first class of the day when my home room teacher stopped me. She smiled sympathetically as she pulled me aside.

"Adam, can I talk to you for a minute?"

"Sure Miss, what's up?" My anxiety bubbled up as we spoke. *What could she want?*

"Well, I was wondering, since you have an IEP (Individual Education Plan), you're eligible to use the special exam room to write your exams. Is that something you wanted to take advantage of?"

My jaw metaphorically hit the floor. Was she implying that I was somehow less capable than others because of my diagnosis? Either way it didn't matter — it wasn't happening.

"Oh..." I stammered at last. "I'm .... I'm okay, thanks anyway Miss."

"Are you sure? It's a resource that's always there for you if you need it."

"I'm positive." I was annoyed that she pressed the issue but did my best not to show it.

"Okay, no problem," she nodded with a smile. "If you change your mind, the offer is always open."

I walked away awkwardly, excited to just get to class and away from her.

I can't believe she even asked, I thought incredulously to myself. *I'm fine. There's nothing wrong with me.*

§

The same thing happened at exam time in June, and then again, every year since. Every semester of high school, my homeroom teacher would ask me if I wanted to take advantage of the provisions in my IEP for extra exam support, and every time I spurned her. I even started to feel a sense of pride at doing so; my success thus far with my exams proved I didn't need help and that they were wrong to ask if I did. At least, that was how I felt.

Of course, the Force (or fate, the universe, what have you) has a way of nudging us all when we get too far off the beaten path, and it certainly did so to me in Grade 11. That year, I took university-level math with Miss Lime, and immediately found myself drowning. I worked so hard to keep up, and yet I just *couldn't*. It was as though there was a mental block preventing me from understanding the concepts my classmates found so easy. I wanted to cry every day, and there was only so much my peers could do to help. My math mark hovered around 50% for most of the semester, and I beat myself up to no end over it. Even though my dad had arranged for a fellow teacher to tutor me (which admittedly did help) I couldn't help but feel like I was sinking fast.

I'm not one of those students who gets 50%, I thought to myself during math one morning as I stared at a test I had just gotten back with yet another low score. My heart pounded.

I'm better than this.

I had metaphorically Hulk smashed my way through preparing for that test, and it *still* wasn't good enough. I felt dejected, defeated, and utterly burned out. Which is why, when my home room teacher did her traditional thing that year and asked me if I wanted to use my IEP to write my exam in the special quiet room with more time, I bit my tongue, hid my tail between my legs, and took her up on the offer. For someone who had long struggled against the knowledge that someone thought I was different and broken somehow, it was a hard thing to do. But barely passing math had my mental health suffering, and I knew I had to do something because the anxiety I felt at utterly tanking was real.

So, one afternoon in mid-June 2005, my home room teacher led me down a long, deserted hallway. After what felt like an eternity, we stopped at a set of double doors being propped open by a doorstop, and she looked over at me once she'd made sure it was the right room.

"Alright, here we are. Remember, you have a whole extra hour to write your math exam Adam, so don't rush. Relax. And good luck."

"Thanks," I nodded quietly and made my way in. Finding a desk in the middle of the room that had been set up for me already, I plopped down into it and pulled out my pencil and eraser.

"Alright Adam," I whispered quietly to myself. "Just get this done and we can go home. Easy enough, right?"

I put my pencil to paper and began writing. I took my time, figuring out each problem to the best of my ability before moving on to the next one. It was still difficult for my brain to do the math thing — that much was unavoidable — but I was surprised by just how much easier it was to process things when there wasn't a time crunch associated with them. It made me think back to the day I spent being evaluated by Sue in Grade 3, or how I failed at timed tests of all stripes throughout the years since. Time was my enemy, it seemed, and the special accommodation room allowed me to fight back against it. It felt like thinking clearly for the first time.

By the end of two hours, I'd finally finished my Math exam in full. Grinning triumphantly, I picked up my test and writing implements, marched to the front of the room, and dropped it proudly on the teacher's desk in the designated spot before strutting out of the room like I owned the place.

I was even prouder when I found out my final mark for the course a few weeks later: 60%. Not only had I passed, but I managed to boost my mark up ten percentage points just by working with a tutor and — most importantly — giving myself some time to breathe while I wrote the final exam.

Okay, okay, I admitted to myself as I left St. Bens on the last day of Grade 11. *I was being too hard on myself for having an IEP. There's nothing wrong with needing extra help sometimes, and I'm really glad I was able to use it when I needed to. Maybe I am one of those people who needs to use his IEP every now and then for some extra support.*

...and maybe... just maybe ... that's perfectly okay after all.

...maybe.

CHAPTER 14

There's an infamous moment in the original *Super Mario Bros.* for NES where, having stormed the castle and beaten Bowser, you're greeted not by Princess Toadstool, but by her assistant Toad instead, whose pixelated eyes lock with yours as he proceeds to tell you "thank you Mario. But our princess is in another castle." In an instant, your jubilant mood deflates somewhat as you realize that you hadn't, in fact, reached the end of your journey — there were still greater challenges ahead, and you couldn't be sure exactly when you'd finally rescue Peach. Obvious 1980s video game misogyny aside, in some ways, this sense of longing yet not knowing exactly how to get to the princess perfectly exemplified what it was like to date in high school as an autistic teenager. I knew stories of knights and princesses weren't appropriate romantic goals to strive for, but I certainly felt Mario's pain all the same.

It actually reminded me a lot of the far newer game *Star Wars: Knights of The Old Republic* by BioWare; every dialogue choice made impacted the outcome in ways that weren't always immediately obvious to me, but that seemed to be well known by everyone else. Dating isn't always the easiest thing for autistic people.

The truth is, I was too busy looking out for my own survival in middle school to look at girls all that much. Once I hit the summer before high school, though, I started longing for romantic companionship. This only intensified once high school began in earnest, and I really started taking note of the girls in my grade. All of a sudden, a whole new world had popped into existence, and I became aware of all the girls around me.

Jedi may have been forbidden romantic attachments by the Jedi Code, but that was one aspect of their teachings I only lived under grudgingly. I desperately wanted to date, but I lacked the confidence and comfort in my own skin needed to ask anyone out.

Because of this, I set out to figure out how to better talk to girls. Unfortunately, my anxiety toward this task was crippling — and that was only online. Doing so face to face seemed almost impossible. In addition, most of what I knew about relationships at that point came from the science fiction movies and TV series I followed. It was hard because I never found myself identifying with the bravado and charisma of typical male protagonists in most stories. I was never *Futurama*'s Zap Brannigan, for example, nor did I really want to be; I identified far more with sensitive, kinder characters like Kif.

For a time, I didn't think I'd find someone to be my girlfriend, so I lived vicariously through my creative writing. I wrote love stories between characters I'd created, and using my vivid imagination, I pictured myself in the scene I was writing, taking part in the romance instead of my characters. In these (frequently fanfiction) stories, I was often the awkward yet heroic protagonist, working alongside the intelligent, commanding, yet subtly sensitive and free-spirited female science officer (Jadzia Dax (*Star Trek: Deep Space Nine*), Dana Scully (*X-Files*), and Captain Janeway (*Star Trek: Voyager*) all came to mind). Oddly enough, this allowed me to practice and flesh out exactly how I would be if-and-when the day finally came I had a relationship of my own.

I wouldn't have to wait long. By the time my third year of high school arrived, I had a small group of friends, was doing well academically, and had found my niche in the social pecking order. That autumn, something big happened though: I took Grade 11 Biology as one of my electives, and in that class I first laid eyes on *her*.

Well ... maybe that wasn't the moment I *first* laid eyes on her ... but it was the moment I first truly *saw* her. Lynn and I had known of each other since Grade 9 and taken French together in Grade 10, but while we definitely connected as friends in that class (and I definitely thought she was cute), we didn't talk much outside school. In the fall of 2004 though, as we sat in Grade 11 Bio, something happened. At first, her interest in me was evidenced only by a sense that I was being observed. One unbearably lazy morning, I looked up from my notes as the teacher droned on about a research project we'd have to write for class, and glanced over at the clock, desperate for the period to end. My eyes never made it to the clock though; as my gaze moved over the front of the room, it landed on Lynn. Our eyes met, and I felt a sharp burst of energy shoot from her rich brown ones to mine. My jaw dropped, but I quickly composed myself.

She seemed interested in me. I was sure of it.

I found myself intrigued. I'd always thought Lynn was cool from our limited interactions — she seemed kind and nerdy. Maybe I could take a chance and get to know her? I decided I would, and when the teacher asked us each to pick a research partner for the assignment, I knew I'd found my chance.

"Hey Lynn," I greeted. I walked over to where she sat with her support worker. She looked up at me and smiled through her thick brown hair.

"Hi Adam," she replied. "Are you here to ask if I want to be your partner?"

"Partner? I ... er ..."

"... You know, for the project?" She laughed and her worker—Miss Dioza— hid a smile behind her hand at my awkwardness and turned away to let us chat.

"Oh. Er ... yeah. Assignment partners. That's right. What

else could I have meant? Um ... do you want to?"

"Absolutely." She nodded. I grinned, taking a seat in the desk beside her extremely high-tech chair. It was a motorized black and silver model, with a plastic tray stretching across her waist. Lynn basically had a mobile desk, and I was impressed.

"So, what made you want to work with me?"

"Honestly? You just seem really nice and I thought it would be fun. I warn you though — I'm a total awkward nerd."

"That's okay, so am I," Lynn countered. "I've been counting the months until *Star Wars: Episode III* comes out. I can't wait!"

My ears perked up.

"You like *Star Wars*?"

"Well yeah ... why? Shouldn't I?"

"No, it's just that ... I guess I'm a little self-conscious about my geeky side."

"I get that," she mused. "I'm so used to people assuming that I'm not smart or with it just because I use this chair and don't move and talk like everyone else. I get a little defensive too."

"I wasn't defensive, I—" I paused and sighed. "But I do know how that feels, in my own way."

"What do you mean?" Lynn's asked. I braced myself as I continued.

"Promise not to tell anyone? I don't really like people knowing without my permission."

"I promise," Lynn nodded. "What is it?"

"Well, when I was a kid, I was diagnosed with something called Asperger's Syndrome. It's basically another name for autism. The doctor said I'd never be able to fall in love or connect with other people or anything. But like ... I dunno ... it's never been a big deal or anything ... I'm just like everyone else and I don't want anyone looking at me differently."

I bowed my head, shocked I'd just opened up to someone after less than a minute of conversation.

"Adam ..."

"What?"

"Look at me."

She was reaching out a hand toward mine. Nervously, I met her half way, and felt a wave of electricity as our skin touched.

"You're not just like everyone else. You always treated me with the same acceptance you show everyone, and not everyone does that. That doctor was full of crap."

I smiled as I looked into her beautiful, warm eyes and felt all my anxiety and awkwardness melt away. *What's happening to me?* I wondered, as I felt my breath go short and struggled to find the words to express what I was feeling.

"Thank you," I finally managed, unsure what else to say. "For what it's worth? I love *Star Wars* too. I can't wait for the new movie either."

"Well then let's get through this assignment," Lynn replied. "Then I want to know if you'd be a Jedi or a Sith."

§

In many ways, Lynn was a kindred spirit, and I think we were brought together by shared experience. We were both, in some ways, outcasts. We were already fast friends, and by December, we talked on the phone every night — about everything from *Star Wars* to history.

I was in love.

More specifically, I was in puppy love. When I was with her, I didn't feel awkward at all; I had more confidence than I knew what to do with! We understood each other completely, and I had never felt as utterly and blissfully happy as I did when we were together.

If I'm being honest with you though, Lynn brought me face to face with a lot of internalized ableism — far more than I even realized in the moment. Up until that point, I wasn't very comfortable at all with the term Asperger's. Sure, I'd started to self-advocate in middle school with the speech competition, but that was one event. On the whole, it was a part of myself that I still wasn't fully ready to face. I'd also picked up lots of toxic stereotypes about disability from the media and mainstream society, and whether I knew it or not, they'd infiltrated my world view as a teenager.

I'm rather ashamed to admit it but fears over what kind of relationship we could possibly have given Lynn being physically disabled started to swirl in my mind. It definitely wasn't one of my better moments, but I was young and naïve, and still had a lot of my own growing to do. The ironic thing is, such fears are the exact same ones people often direct at those of us who are autistic. "What kind of life could they possibly have?" Some ask. Others lament how their children will forever be trapped within their own minds without early intervention and potentially harmful therapies. The hurtful stereotypes around disability in general and autism in particular are real, and in Grade 11, I fell for them hook, line, and sinker.

Because of all of this anxiety, nothing more than friendship ever actually happened between Lynn and I. Through no fault of her own, she'd been yet again faced with the spectre of ableism through my own insecurities. It wasn't fair to her, and it breaks my heart to this day that I handled it as poorly as I did. When the moment came for us to become something more than friends, I told her I couldn't take that next step. We drifted apart somewhat not long after, and I grew to feel very awkward around her. I was consumed by guilt and ashamed that I'd allowed my own internalized feelings of inadequacy and ableism to get in my way of asking her out more formally.

It may not have been an official breakup, but it sure felt like one. I tried to drown my feelings of guilt and sadness in my hobbies — video games, writing, even school work — but ultimately, my self-inflicted heartbreak and feelings of moral failure had to heal on their own over time.

Eventually, I did apologize to Lynn for everything. I don't remember the exact details of the conversation, but I know we ultimately patched things up as best we could. In Grade 12, we even managed to rekindle our friendship to somewhere close to what it was before things got complicated. It made my heart happy to no end that we'd been able to do so, but I didn't take the hard lessons of the situation laying down either. I knew I'd have to do better going forward and start to confront some of that ingrained prejudice that had gotten in my way. It was an extremely hard lesson to learn, but I'm glad I did all the same.

And before you ask, yes, we did get to watch *Star Wars Episode III: Revenge of the Sith* together one night in senior year. We were both gutted by Anakin's turn to the dark side at the end of the film, no matter how much we both knew it was coming. As I look back on my relationship with Lynn now, I'm really happy I was able to avoid a similar fate. If confronting the darkness within was a key tenet of the Jedi path, then Lynn marked a point in my life where I started to do just that.

§

Early in Grade 12, I found myself with another crush — her name was Kara and we'd met randomly over lunch one day, when she and her friends invited Chris and me to sit with them. They were weirdos and freaks, like us, though in a different way; they were goth/punk/emo kids obsessed with anime, with black hair and piercings. After a few weeks of lunches together, Kara and I grew closer.

"So ... what are you doing this weekend?"

Kara looked at me intensely from across the table; her long black hair falling to her shoulders. Awkwardly, I shovelled a forkful of Caesar salad into my mouth.

"Um ... nothing really ... why?" I mumbled through the lettuce.

"Great. Then you should come to my party on Friday night."

Me? A party? My eyes went wide as I processed the request.

"You want ... *me* ... to go to your party? Really?"

"Yeah," confirmed Kara. "It'll be fun. We'll be playing *Mario Kart*, and doing other stuff ... Chris already said he'd come."

"When did you even get to ask him?" I questioned, confused. Regardless, if Chris had already committed to going, that was one more person I knew who would be there. Plus, it *did* sound fun.

"Alright, sure," I agreed. "I mean, I'm never one to turn down a game of *Mario Kart. Double Dash*, I'm guessing?"

"Of course. I don't have anything but a GameCube." Kara's eyes narrowed as she grinned at me. "We aren't all big cute dorks like you."

Did ... did she just call me cute? I was flummoxed but didn't get a chance to ask because we'd already moved on to other topics. I shrugged it off and read no further into it. *We're friends and gaming is fun*, I reasoned, my typical autistic obliviousness kicking in. I had no suspicions that there was any deeper motivation to either Kara's invite, or her use of the word cute to describe me.

Friday after school, my dad gave me a ride to Kara's. She lived in a geared-to-income townhouse complex not overly far from where we lived. It was walkable but far enough to make it annoying. Climbing out of our grey Jeep, I walked up to the front door and raised my hand to knock, only for Marie to open it before my fist even made contact.

Marie was one of Kara's friends, albeit the one I knew the least. She was the quiet one at our table and always kept to herself.

"Oh ... Hi Adam ...," Marie greeted me awkwardly, her gaze dropping to the floor as I entered. Her long brown hair was tied in a ponytail that hung limply down her back.

"Hi Marie ... Kara didn't tell me you'd be here."

"Is that a problem?" Marie flashed a smile, resting the palm of her hand on her waist. I was afraid I'd said something wrong, and my anxiety spiked.

"Oh ... no! Not at all. I'm actually .... happy ... to see you," I ventured.

"Good," she giggled. "You can 'see' me kick your butt at *Mario Kart*."

Marie led me upstairs, occasionally looking back at me mischievously. Chris was already in Kara's small bedroom; her blue double bed was a mess of blankets and pillows, and it was pushed up against the right wall, taking up most of the space.

There was a sliver of ground between the edge of the bed and the other wall where a short bookshelf was set up, along with Kara's small, tube TV. Her purple Nintendo GameCube was hooked up alongside it, and the empty case belonging to *Mario Kart: Double Dash* lay open in front. We sat down beside the bookshelf.

"Hey Adam, nice of you to finally show up." Kara chuckled as she climbed over her bed to get to the GameCube and power it on. The logo appeared and the game began to load.

"Are you ready for this, Merdy?" Chris joked, and I nodded. I was ready alright. Everyone was going down.

We played four-player *Mario Kart* for a couple hours, only pausing long enough to banter playfully and choose new characters. I stuck with the iconic Mario and Luigi duo as my playable characters. What can I say? As an autistic person, I enjoy the comfort of familiarity and sameness. I've played as Mario in every *Mario Kart* game since *Mario Kart 64*, and I wasn't about to change things up now. I even did pretty decently, though I had to admit Kara clobbered me — she was *good*.

After a particularly annoying winning streak on the part of our hostess, I was about ready to throw my controller in frustration. Thankfully, the group as a whole decided to take a break from video games, and everyone started making suggestions about what we should do next.

"How about truth or dare," Kara suggested, shrugging in a way that tried to say "nonchalant" but had probably been rehearsed first.

Truth or dare: destroyer of friendships, creator of awkward teenage moments. With Marie and me sitting side-by-side on the floor still, and Chris and Kara on the bed looking down at us, we took turns going clockwise around the group. Chris began, looking over at Kara:

"Alright, truth — what's the most disgusting thing you've ever done?"

Kara rolled her eyes as Chris chuckled to himself, evidently highly amused.

"Probably the time I walked in on Mr. Iroh kissing Miss Lime in the teacher's lounge."

"Oh come on that didn't really happen ... did it?" I scoffed. Kara narrowed her eyes cryptically.

"That's all you'll get out of me about it." She laughed. Chris and I knew better than to press further.

When Kara's turn came next, things got interesting. Looking straight at Marie, she uttered her challenge:

"Truth or dare, Marie."

"Dare."

We all gasped. No one *ever* chose dare. Giving someone that kind of power over you — especially in this game — was so high risk you were either brave or foolish to even try it. I wasn't quite sure at the moment exactly which of the two Marie was, but none of us would have to wait long to find out.

"Alright," Kara said haltingly, momentarily thrown off by the surprise. "Um ... Oh. I know. I dare you to do the first thing you think of to the person next to you."

I wasn't sure Kara knew exactly what she was doing when she said that, but I *was* entirely sure she didn't expect what happened next. After all, the first thought on someone's mind could be a lot of things: Slap, tickle, hug ... a million other options.

Marie did none of these. She looked over at me and after a moment's hesitation leaned in, kissing me squarely, and lingering for a few moments as our lips locked. It was as though time slowed to a crawl. I was floored.

Is this really happening?

I was taken aback, unsure how to feel. Shocked? Confused? Terrified? I had never given it much thought, but it's clear to me in retrospect that on some level I felt as though moments like these were out of reach for someone like me. I saw my peers doing things like kissing and sharing intimate moments, but doubted I'd ever be able to partake in the experience. I never consciously connected that feeling with Asperger's, but it definitely played a part all the same. The invisible wall yet again stood between me and a normal teenage social experience, or so it seemed at the time. Marie kissing me that night changed the game. The wall began to melt away, replaced by a bubbling and happy feeling in my chest. Bliss. This was my first kiss. And while I might have appreciated some notice and an opportunity to say no, I didn't complain either.

She liked me. She really liked me. More importantly, she *kissed* me! Maybe I *could* have nice things like that with someone after all.

My eyes widened as we pulled out of the kiss at last. Marie smiled bashfully, suddenly shy about what had just happened. Chris and Kara were both shocked too, though had I been more aware in the moment, I might have noticed Kara's look of utter indignation. Unfortunately, my autistic brain has never been fantastic at reading social situations like these, and so all of this went right over my head. I later learned Kara had orchestrated the party to get closer to me, and when Marie had opted for dare instead of truth, it forced Kara to improvise. Clearly, she hadn't thought her challenge through.

"Whoa!" Chris finally exclaimed, breaking the awkward silence. "That got intense, fast. Okay, who's turn is it next?"

The night continued for several more hours (and a brief return to *Mario Kart*) before my dad finally came to pick me up. The whole time, I was consumed with thoughts of Marie and what had happened. I had never really considered Marie in that way before … which seemed to be true of most social situations I found myself in. I realized then and there just how many experience points I apparently still needed to dump into my Perception trait and sighed.

But even still, Marie *was* cute, and smart, and we got along well. *I don't know,* I thought to myself. *Maybe I should see where this goes?*

Being autistic in this kind of situation is tricky. Because of my historic naïveté around relationships, I have always tended to throw myself all in when someone expressed interest, and that started here with Marie. In the first few weeks of our relationship, I felt extremely enthusiastic and wanted to spend every moment kissing her. It was a new experience, and because of my hyper-sensitivity to all kinds of sensory experiences, the incredible feelings I got as we locked lips were heightened immeasurably. Every touch was more intense than any I'd felt before. Every kiss more heart-pounding.

It was one of the most intense moments of my young life. And yet, I also couldn't shake the feeling that something was wrong. Part of it may have been burning out — we neurodivergent folks tend to do that after a short time because strong sensory and emotional experiences can be exhausting — but there was also more to it than that. It was as though there was a war in my brain between the rational and emotional sides of my consciousness. Physically and emotionally, I was strongly drawn to Marie. Rationally, however, my autistic sense of perfectionism and rigidity conflicted with this. I overanalyzed every problem and flaw in our relationship, and it nagged at me even though I tried not to let it. She was sweet and kind, and we were extremely attracted to each other. That should have been enough, shouldn't it?

As our relationship progressed, I came to realize what it was that was making me feel uncomfortable. Marie struggled with untreated depression, and because of how I threw all-in emotionally with her, it put a strain on our relationship because I started to make her feelings *my* feelings.

In addition to experiencing my own emotions deeply, I've also always been able to pick up on the emotional states of others, even if I can't for the life of me grasp the reasoning behind them most of the time. If I think about it now, being autistic definitely contributes to this because of how I've always struggled with regulating my feelings. It's like using the X-Ray mode on the Farsight XR-20 in *Perfect Dark* for Nintendo 64; you can see every other player on the map, but not the walls and other obstacles blocking off your access to them. Of course, while this was by design in Rare's classic first person shooter (seriously, it's easily the cheapest weapon in the game), as someone on the autistic spectrum, it didn't always work that way for me in real life. Because of this, I found dating Marie very difficult. On the one hand, I was empathetic and wanted to help her, on the other, I found it frequently sucked up all my energy to do so. I was often frustrated I couldn't do more. It never occurred to me that I wasn't responsible, or capable, of giving Marie the support she needed. On some level, I think I felt as though I wanted to do better than I had with Lynn and so tried to be there for her as best I could. Unfortunately, by trying to do so, I often made it worse. Things ultimately came to a head and got quite toxic between us, and that was when my parents told me I would have to take care of myself first.

And so, after a four-month relationship, I did.

Marie and I broke up not long after, though had to deal with each other for the rest of the year because of our interconnected social group. Eventually, a tenuous friendship emerged from this awkward period of forced contact, but it was still very shaky and uncomfortable. Even so, I sighed in relief, happy that at least things had stopped being quite as tense between us.

The thing about dating in high school as an autistic person is that it can be a dangerous wasteland of trials and tribulations. It can also, however, be a key cornerstone in social development. That's what it was for me. Both Lynn and Marie taught me different lessons about dating and relationships, and while they couldn't be more different, they also helped shape my social outlook. I learned from Lynn how thrilling love and romance could be while also gaining an awareness of my weaknesses and assumptions, while from Marie I learned that looking after your own mental health in a relationship can ultimately help the other person's. Though neither of the relationships lasted, their legacies persisted.

Even if my princess hadn't proven to be in the St. Bens castle after all, I had at least gotten through the most awkward of teenage dating moments in one piece and grown a tad wiser for it.

CHAPTER 15

With teenage romance checked off my list of adolescent experiences, I moved onto the next one: employment. Much like dating, work is something that doesn't always come easily to those of us on the spectrum. Some of us have difficulty working at all — the stimulation can be overwhelming, to say nothing of the unclear social rules and unfortunate lack of understanding and accommodations in many workplaces — while others can work, but struggle in different ways. The crux of it is that work can be one of the hardest things a spectrum dweller has to face in life, yet it can also be one of the most essential. It's certainly not the only path you can take, and many of my fellow members of the autistic community have found other ways to secure their independence aside from working a typical nine-to-five job. Indeed, the one thing most working autistic adults have in common is that in some way, shape, or form, we've all found our niche. That one place, occupation, or monetized passion that embraces our talents and lets us be ourselves. After all, too often, we place excessive focus on forcing people with diverse needs into the traditional productivity paradigm, when the goal should be helping people find the path that works best for *them* as individuals.

I can't speak for anyone's experiences except my own in this regard but, trust me when I say, while I've never lacked the ability to work, it has always been situational depending on the job in question and even when a workplace did suit me, it was often still an internal battle. In many ways, I owe my work ethic to Trish. Despite our at-times difficult relationship, she never infantilized me, presumed incompetence, or let me back away from things I thought I couldn't do. My first job was no different in this regard.

"You can't keep sitting around every day playing video games, Adam."

Yet another dinnertime debate, this time as we ate breaded chicken cutlets my Nona had made. And asparagus. I've never liked asparagus; the sickly green colour, bumpy texture, and smell instantly sets off my gag reflex. Autistic sensory hypersensitivities are fun like that. Ella and my other siblings — Amelia and Mark — ate it up, but I remained just as wary of it as ever.

"You're seventeen. You should be working, making money."

A job? What? But ... what about my summer? I didn't want to give up my freedom—I liked things as they were dammit. Concerns I didn't hesitate to make known.

"But ... I need my summer," I insisted. "I need down time and time to see friends. I don't want to work."

As we spoke, my little brother Mark grabbed two breadsticks and began drumming on the side of his plate while mumbling movie quotes to himself under his breath. A habit we shared. Ella scowled at him and told him to stop, while Amelia seemed more upset he'd taken the last two breadsticks.

"Do you know how many others are working at your age? Probably most of them." Trish paused for a moment to think. "I started working in my dad's convenience store when I was sixteen. It's good for you — it builds character."

I nodded nervously, not sure what else to say. When Trish got an idea in her head, it was difficult bordering on impossible to get her to drop it. Silently, I resigned myself to the fact that I'd be getting a job.

At least I'll make money from it. I thought to myself, trying to find a silver lining. *That will be nice.*

§

That weekend, I went to a job fair hosted by the local YMCA. It was crowded and nerve-wracking, but I strove to play it as cool as I could. We had just learned how to write resumes that year and getting to practice selling myself was a muscle I enjoyed flexing, no matter how nervous it made me (or how terrible I probably was at it in retrospect). In some ways, it was like choosing a job class in *Final Fantasy*, except as a teenager, I wasn't a high enough level to qualify for anything truly interesting. After wandering around a gymnasium packed with other students and people looking for jobs for what felt like hours, I handed out a few resumes, and headed home. I forgot all about it for the rest of the weekend.

I'd set the wheels in motion though, and while I made little of it, clearly someone had. I got a call that Monday from a woman asking for me specifically. I was being offered a job. It was a summer student landscaping position with a property management company, and truth be told ... it sounded absolutely awful right from the get-go. As much as I wanted to say no and go back to having a peaceful summer, I knew what Trish and my dad would say if I did, so with great hesitation, I accepted the offer.

"That's great news," Trish said when I told her.

"It's going to be a good experience for you," added my dad.

"Yeah," I said. Internally, I want to scream and say: "No. I'm not going to do it." Unfortunately, I knew screaming like that wouldn't be viewed positively by my parents. Not to mention, it probably wouldn't end well given how volatile Trish and I could be with each other. So, I nodded and braced myself for the inevitable.

That last night of freedom before I started my new job felt like walking the plank; every hour I was one step closer to plunging deep into unknown, hazard-riddled waters. Mitch and I spent the evening hanging out playing video games and drinking too much Pepsi. It was something we always did, but it felt *different* somehow — as though the dream was truly over.

"So, are you nervous?" He asked. I cringed a little as I thought about it.

"A little yeah," I replied. "I mean, I've never done this before."

"I know, but it really won't be that bad. I've had summer jobs most of high school. I mean, mine were tutoring, not breaking my back in the hot sun ..."

"Not helping dude."

"Sorry, sorry," Mitch said. "But if it makes you feel better, you can come over here after work and complain if you need to."

"I know, thanks dude." I forced my face into a fake half-smile. "I appreciate it."

"Anytime. Hey, let me go see if my dad's back—maybe I can borrow the car and we can go grab snacks and tech magazines at Shoppers?"

"Sounds good."

Despite Mitch's efforts, I was still extremely nervous, though I now also found myself — to some degree — looking forward to starting — it *was* my first job after all, and disposable income would be nice. *Maybe*, I thought. *Maybe it wouldn't be as bad as I was expecting. After all, lots of people have jobs, right?*

§

It actually *was* that bad. I remember it well: I woke up at the ungodly hour of 6 a.m., already in a bad mood. Struggling, I made my way upstairs, poured a bowl of cereal, and worked hard to force my bleary eyes open. I probably should have started drinking coffee right then and there. Not long after I'd settled in, my dad walked into the room, beaming as he laid eyes on me.

"There he is." He walked over and clasped my shoulder, smiling proudly. "How's the working boy? All ready for your first day?"

I'm not exactly sure the precise words I used, but I'm fairly certain my sleep-deprived-still-tired brain strung together something that sounded a little like a cross between a snoring

old man and a dog growl. Think: "BLARGHSFDSKDSFD."
My dad was amused.

"You'll be fine. It builds character! I still remember my first
job at Woolco way back in the sixties ..."

My dad has always been prone to telling long-winded
stories with morals attached to them. They'd always start with
some anecdote about his childhood or young adult life, and
eventually — after several minutes — segue into why x/y/z
situation was good for me, my two sisters, or my brother.
Sometimes we'd even get the "you kids don't know how good
you've got it" rant, followed by talk of how Nono and Nona
would never have put up with it. That was usually when any
one of us got in trouble for whatever reason. Thankfully, that
morning he spared me a long story and kept things short.

"I know, I know Dad." I groaned as I shovelled more Fruit
Loops into my mouth. I so wasn't ready for this; I was covered
in a cold sweat and couldn't stop thinking about how the
day would go. A few minutes after my dad, Trish came down,
smiling as she noticed me in my work clothes. She was dressed
in work clothes of her own: a pair of blue dress pants and a blue
blazer with gold accent buttons worn over a white dress shirt.
Her newly dyed blond hair was smartly combed and styled as it
hung at shoulder length. All told, she looked very professional
and in charge ... which was probably the whole point as she was
sitting in on school board job interviews that day.

"Ready to go Adam?"

"Ugh," I grumbled as I got up and put my bowl away.
"Yeah."

"Let's go then."

We had to drive all the way across town to get to the
worksite I was reporting to, and along the way, I was silent,
absorbed in my thoughts. Sensing my nervousness, Trish spoke
at last.

"It's going to be fine, you'll see. I made you a few pizza subs
for lunch just to get you through the day."

I smiled slightly. Pizza subs were (and are) one of my favourite foods, and for Trish to have made some for me? Well, I appreciated the gesture. It would definitely make the day far less terrible.

"Thanks Mum," I replied, looking over at her. She smiled back and nodded as she drove.

"Want some Tim Hortons on our way?"

§

When I finally got to the job site, I was emotionally overwhelmed by a mixture of trepidation, excitement, and outright dread. My body trembled and my mind spun rapidly down the anxiety rabbit hole. Steeling myself as best I could, I climbed out of the Jeep and made my way over to my new boss. He was a scrawny, lanky man of medium height. His skin was leathery, his hair a dark, greasy brown, and his eyes looked beady and sunken in his bony face. He reminded me of the Crypt Keeper.

"You Adam?" I nodded nervously, looking back at Trish, who smiled and urged me on. Clutching my lunch cooler in one hand so hard the sweat made it slip in my grip, I moved closer.

"Hmmmm ...," He began, grunting as he gave me a once-over. "Name's Pudding. Roger Pudding. You'll do what I say, when I say it. Got it?"

"O-okay," I stammered. He looked over at Trish in her vehicle, then back at me.

"That your mom?"

"Yeah," I replied. Roger furrowed his brow and smirked.

"Go back over there and tell her to be here to pick you up at four. We'll be done by then."

I nodded and ran back over to Trish's idling jeep. She rolled down the window.

"Think you're going to live?"

"Yeah," I replied. "He's kinda sleazy though. He said we should be done by four."

"Okay I'll be back here to pick you up then," Trish said. "Good luck!"

With that, she pulled away, leaving me alone in the parking lot with the delightful Mr. Pudding.

Whelp, I thought, sighing. *Here we go.*

I turned on my heel and walked slowly back toward Roger, who had moved over to his red flatbed Chevy Avalanche.

"Mom or stepmom?" The question seemed odd, but in typical autistic fashion, I made nothing of it and replied honestly.

"Stepmom, but she's been around since I was really little."

"Well hot damn she's a milf," Roger continued, chuckling. "Know what a milf is, kid?"

"Um ...," I legitimately did not know how to respond to his question. Seeing my lack of understanding, Roger groaned.

"Mother I'd like to f —" he began, and then cut himself short. "Aw you know what? They don't teach you kids anything these days. Come on let's go."

As we climbed into the cabin of his truck, my brain began to process the situation. I was shocked and horrified by what he had just said. That was my stepmom he was talking about like a piece of meat. It was disgusting. It was gross. It was shameful, and disrespectful, and ... and it was only the beginning.

§

Working with Roger was a hellish ordeal. I couldn't relate to him in any way; he was rude and crass, his humour wasn't funny to me in the slightest, and the worst part was, I often couldn't tell if he was joking about something or being serious. Roger basically intensified every challenging part of being autistic, while the repetitive, unstimulating nature of the landscaping job we did diminished any of the positives to near nothingness. By the end of the first day, I had reached a clear decision — this job class wasn't working for me. I was going to quit. After all, it was easy enough to do in most RPGs, and exploring your skills and weaknesses is important. You can't just settle for the first job that comes your way. Surely, Trish and my dad would understand, right?

§

"You're not quitting." Trish stood firm as we drove home. Ironically, the tune blasting from the Jeep's speakers was *So You Had a Bad Day*.

You don't know the half of it, I remember thinking.

"Why not? I'm miserable there. Roger is really creepy, and kind of a jerk. And I hate the job. No paycheque is worth this ..."

"Adam you can't just quit when a job gets tough. That's not how real life works."

"Yeah, but ..."

"But what?" Trish glanced over at me while we were stopped at a red light. I calmed myself to respond.

"It's exhausting, I smell, and it's just the worst."

"Do you honestly think any job doesn't have those things, Adam?" Trish began, turning her head and accelerating as the light turned green. "My job is ten times more stressful. I walked into a school where I wasn't taken seriously and turned things around. I deal with challenging kids from some of the roughest parts of town on an everyday basis. Do you think I want to get up every morning and go in to face all of that?"

She definitely had a point. Trish was the principal at one of our city's biggest high schools, and things hadn't been easy for her when she'd first passed through its front doors. Everyone had their own ideas about how the school should be run, and it had taken her years to force through changes, iron out wrinkles, and take control of the situation.

"No," I mustered at last.

"No, I don't. But I do anyway, and that's what life is all about sometimes. Sucking it up, pulling yourself up off the ground, and just doing it. You know ... like the Nike logo?"

"Just do it?"

"Just DOOO it!"

It didn't happen all the time, but Trish had a silly side that revelled in dumb jokes and potty humour. It appeared we'd transitioned into that territory. It was a far happier place to be, and I started laughing in spite of myself.

"So tomorrow, what are you going to do?"

"I'm going to go in there and just do it. But ... you should know something."

"What's up?"

"Well," I began, still shocked by the whole thing myself. "Roger ... he ... uh ... called you a milf."

Trish's eyes widened. We drove in silence for a minute or two longer before she turned to look at me, groaning:

"What a fucking pig."

§

As the days went on, I gradually found myself developing a routine — the all-too-important coping tool that most of us on the autistic spectrum rely on. Landscaping was probably the worst fit imaginable for me as a job — it was tedious, repetitive, and it felt like the work was never done — but at least I started getting used to it. Roger, on the other hand, took every opportunity he could to berate me. I still remember the first time we were sweeping an empty apartment bedroom: he handed me the broom and asked me to clean up while he checked something for the owner nearby. Before long, he shook his head and stomped back over.

"You call that sweeping kid?"

"I ... er ..."

"Nevermind," he replied harshly, cutting me off and grabbing the broom from my hands. My skin took on that tingly, slightly rubbery "I don't belong in this body" feeling I always got when I felt extremely awkward. I wasn't sure exactly what I'd done to upset the man this time. Roger aggressively swept and cursed at me as he worked.

"Like this see?" He said as he demonstrated. "Like this. Jeezus fucking Christ kid, have you never swept before? LIKE

THIS!"

I stood there feeling uncomfortable, but not knowing how to fix the situation and do better. As an autistic person, I can be clumsy and physically awkward. It made the whole experience far more difficult than it should have been.

"Aw hell, nevermind," Roger groaned as he shoved the broom back at me. "Finish this up. You can do that ... right?"

"Uh ... yeah ..."

"Good." He moved toward the door, calling out to my co-worker, John.

"Hey John. The kid's sweeping. Wanna go for a smoke? This is gonna be a while."

My heart sank as his footfalls bounded away and out of the room.

I hate this job.

§

The weeks dragged on, and I found myself counting the days until the end of summer. Roger and his buddy John had taken to making fun of me whenever they could, such that I typically spent my lunch hours eating alone, as far from them as I could get. They weren't deterred by that; they often found other ways to get to me at those times. Like the day they decided to throw French fries at me while I was eating, taunting that I'd be in the unemployment line after this. It was a miserable experience, but one day toward the end of summer in particular still stands out in my mind — both as an example of how terrible the job was, and how it brought out my autistic traits in full force.

On a hot, hazy day in late August 2005, we'd been sent to tidy up the soil around the bases of the rows and rows of tiny trees and bushes that lined the road leading up to one of the company's apartment buildings. Simple enough, right? Roger certainly thought so, and he handed me a shovel and told me to get to work on a section of trees down the road. The autistic brain is a funny thing, though; it often sees things in an extremely logical way, but it doesn't always see them in the most expected way. Most people, when given such a task, would probably try to copy how the existing tree bases looked to keep things nice and uniform. Round bases are elegant in a way, aren't they? Naturally, I had to do things differently. When I looked at the messy section of trees to which I'd been assigned, it dawned on me that it would be far easier to maintain this shrubbery if the holes at the base of the trees were square, not round. That way, they could be dug uniformly and cleaned up more efficiently. It didn't occur to me that perhaps the owners didn't want the holes square. Perhaps they even expected them dug the same way the others had already been done. Roger hadn't specified, after all—he'd simply told me to dig the holes and clear the undergrowth — so I figured I'd do my job in the best, most efficient way possible. It all made sense to me, so with as much eagerness as I could muster for the repetitive, menial task, I got to work.

Several hours passed as I worked tidying the soil patches into neat, square-shaped troughs. I was starting to feel genuinely proud of myself and my efforts. At least, as much as I could given how much I hated that job. Roger had finished his section and was making his way over to check on my progress when he stopped dead in his tracks — mouth agape, eyes wide, and brow twitching.

"What the fuck did you do?" Confused, I looked at him.

"I cleaned the tree bases up," I began defensively. "Like you told me to?"

"CHRIST KID. They're ...they're ... SQUARE!"

"Yep. I figured it made more sen—"

"You figured?" Roger interrupted, raising his voice. "Oh, you *figured* alright. How long do you *figure* it's going to take us to fix up your fuckup?"

I blanched.

"I ... er ..."

"I mean *geez* kid. All the *other* ones were round. Why would you start making these *square*? How does *that* make sense?"

I wanted to tell him to shut up, to stop berating me, to explain how, in fact, a square hole actually made far more sense from a maintenance perspective. Not to mention it still looked really good. Unfortunately, I was speechless with anxiety: my throat dry and my mouth silent. Absolutely nothing I said would make the situation better, so I just stood there and took his abuse.

"You know what? Give me that shovel. Go help John get more rocks." His eyes narrowed as he glared at me.

"You *can* do that right ... can't you kid?"

I nodded silently, feeling like absolute garbage as I shuffled away. I only knew one thing (or rather, three closely related things) for sure: I hated him. I hated the job. I hated the whole damn experience.

§

I counted down the days as September approached, and with it a return to school and an end to Roger. When the last day finally ended — the longest eight hours of my life — I jumped for joy. It was a huge relief — I felt as light as a feather — and those last few days of summer before I started my senior year of high school were among the best I'd ever had. I'd survived.

You could make the case that I *should* have quit: Roger was an abusive bully, and no one should have to endure that. I was uniquely well-equipped in that I had support from my family, and my stubborn sense of determination allowed me to find coping mechanisms and survive the summer ... if just barely. For other people, and especially other autistic people, bosses like Roger are just one part of what makes it so difficult to find and sustain "regular" employment. Just because I stuck with it doesn't mean anyone else could, or should, have. A person's worth isn't defined by their ability to work, so I'd never tell anyone else to "suck it up and deal with it."

And yet, oddly, I'm actually glad I fought through it and didn't quit. It taught me not to give up in the face of insurmountable odds, and as Trish says, "Everyone has a job they've hated. It's those jobs that teach us to appreciate the good ones we get later, to work hard, and pick our battles wisely." Years later, when I found myself working at Blockbuster Video while in university and loving every minute of it (because who wouldn't love having bosses that respect and trust you, hanging out with fellow nerds and getting ten free movie or game rentals per week?) I realized she was right.

Say what you will about the "Roger Experience"; it certainly had an effect on me.

CHAPTER 16

Jobs weren't limited purely to part-time work, however, and this was something I confronted in my final year of high school. After all, most epic adventures have a moment where the hero is faced with a choice that will seal their fate, and with the end of Grade 12 in sight, I found myself grappling with my own such important question; what did I want to do with my life? Truthfully, I'd always known, although it didn't make for the easiest path forward.

I wanted to be a writer.

Being both autistic and ADHD means, in my experience, that my brain is always going. It wanders and jumps from topic to topic on a train of thought so fast that it's often well ahead of my ability to articulate what I'm thinking out loud. Because of this, while I am considered intelligent by most traditional measures, I also tend to be clumsy and socially awkward with my speech. Words will escape me, or I will fumble trying to express a relatively obvious thought. This doesn't happen when I'm writing though. I feel liberated when I write. It's as though my mind can soar through the multiverse, visit alien worlds, and express millions of ideas with an ease not afforded when I'm speaking out loud. Writing sets me free, and as such, pursuing a career related to it seemed like a natural fit. I did a co-op placement in Grade 11 at our local newspaper, *The Sudbury Star*, where I'd gotten a lot of praise from some of the more seasoned writers for my work. I'd even caught the eye of Nintendo with an article I wrote about the Nintendo DS, and they offered to send me review copies of games in exchange for articles written about them. Yeah, that was pretty cool. It made my nerdy little heart extremely happy.

With all of that literary success under my belt, the next step on my quest seemed logical; I planned to apply to Cambrian College's Journalism program and earn a diploma, then find a job writing for a newspaper somewhere. I liked the plan, it was comfortable, and I felt confident in it. There was just one problem; the job market for journalists in print media was changing wildly in the mid-to-late 2000s with the rise of the internet, and journalism was no longer a field that had a lot of job security. All of these concerns were points Trish and my dad brought up to me one evening as we were having dinner at East Side Mario's.

"I'm just not sure it's a good move, Adam," Trish said. I looked at her across the table and frowned.

"But why? I really want to give it a shot," I replied. "Besides, I highly doubt newspapers are going anywhere. They might change to digital, but they'll still be around."

"You're probably right, Adam," my dad added, "but at the same time, we don't know that for sure. Besides, even if they stick around, companies will probably use this as an excuse to downsize. They may not hire as many journalists, and then your diploma wouldn't get you very far at all."

I paused as I considered this. Could my dad and Trish be right? I didn't love what they were saying, but they had a point, and I admitted as much to them.

"Fair enough," I said, feeling somewhat dejected. "But then, what would you guys do?"

Trish smiled as she looked me in the eyes. "Have you considered going into teaching?"

I scowled. Not this again. Trish and my dad had a tendency to want to push all of us into teaching. They were biased, of course, being in the field themselves. In their minds, teaching had good benefits, a pension, a good salary, and great holidays. It was hard to fault them for thinking all of that, and yet something about it sat the wrong way with me all the same. I wanted to chart my own path, not be beholden to the achievements and opinions of my parents.

Even still, I did want to go to university too. My Grade 11 history teacher Mr. McClane had awakened my passion for the subject a year or so before, and truth be told, I did want to continue my studies in that field. I loved the thought of studying history in university. Maybe I'd even get a Master's in it some day?

"You're really determined to get me to say yes to that, aren't you?" I asked Trish at last. She nodded.

"It *really* is an amazing job Adam," she said. "Besides, nothing says you *have* to teach after you graduate, it would just be a better set of credentials to have than a journalism diploma in this job market. You know what I mean?"

"Yeah," I confirmed, pondering it for a moment. Finally, I looked back up at her and my dad as I took a sip from my iced tea.

"Okay, what the heck, I'll do it. But I want to study history as my major."

"I think that's a great idea," my dad commented. "I'm glad you see things our way."

"Me too," I said half-heartedly, feeling my heart sinking a little as I agreed. It wasn't that I didn't like the plan; I did. I was very happy about the prospect of studying history. I just wasn't sold on the teaching part. Despite that, I decided to keep an open mind, and as we moved on with our meal, I even found myself getting a little excited about the whole thing.

Now all I needed to do was start applying.

§

It was a cold Friday in late April of 2006 when I received my acceptance letter to Laurentian University, and I was beside myself with excitement. I had done it; I had made it into post-secondary school. As well, Laurentian was a local school, which meant I didn't need to deal with the stress of moving away — something my parents didn't think I'd be ready for. I disagreed with them of course, but all the same, it was hard to argue with the thrill of being accepted. Not only that — I had also earned a $2000 scholarship in the process. To say I was proud would be an understatement.

"Dear Mr. Mardero," I read the letter aloud as Marie walked beside me to our bus at the end of the day. We had managed to eke out a friendship by the time my letter came in, and I was thrilled to get to share it with her. "Thank you for your interest in Laurentian University. We are pleased to offer you acceptance to the Concurrent Education Program for the 2006/2007 academic year."

"That's really exciting Adam," Marie exclaimed. "Congratulations! How does it feel?"

"Awesome," I replied, grinning ear to ear. I still wasn't entirely sold on taking a teaching degree, but it was hard to argue with getting into university.

"Don't people call Laurentian 'last chance university' though?" Marie smirked and punched me teasingly. I scoffed.

"That's just a silly joke," I said. "Besides, they have good programs."

"I know, I know," she answered. "I'm really happy for you Adam."

"Thanks," I smiled back at her slightly awkwardly. "Hey, I know things have been a little uncomfortable between us this year ..."

"Don't even worry about it," she replied. "I'll live. I'm just glad we still get to be friends."

"We definitely do," I said. "I'm happy about that too."

"So have you considered who you're taking to prom?" Marie cocked an eyebrow inquisitively. I sighed.

"That's still so far away," I began. She shook her head admonishingly.

"They're already selling tickets. You kind of need to think about this."

"Well, I *was* considering asking Kara," I said, feeling uncomfortable as I admitted this. "That is ... if you're okay with that. She's your best friend, and after everything between us, I'd totally understand if you said no."

"It's totally cool, I promise Adam," Marie commented. "Besides, I know she's been hoping you'd ask her."

"She has?" I asked. Marie nodded.

"Looks like me messing up her game night plans with you didn't really dissuade her after all, huh?" She smirked mischievously.

"Are you surprised? It's Kara we're talking about." I took a deep breath as we spoke, anxiety rising at the prospect of it. Kara and me? At prom? The thought sounded amazing.

"Look Adam, all I'm saying is you should ask her sooner than later," Marie advised. "She won't wait around forever."

"Yeah," I confirmed, feeling galvanized and inspired as we boarded our bus and headed to our respective homes. Marie was right, and after all, I'd just gotten accepted to university; surely, I could stretch my luck a little further and go two for two?

§

The end of high school came like a whirlwind; fast and frantic, and over before I realized it. After my conversation with Marie, I did in fact ask Kara to the graduation dance — a request she accepted eagerly. And so, on a hot summer night in mid-June of 2006, my dad drove the two of us to the hall St. Bens had rented for our prom. I had a lot of anxiety around leaving high school; I'd done a lot of healing and growing in equal measure there, and while starting university was a big new adventure in itself, I was sad to be leaving St. Bens behind. I found myself lost in thought about this as Kara and I made our way to the dance.

Nevertheless, just because I was nervous didn't mean I wasn't also thrilled by my immediate future that night. Me and Kara, dancing with all our friends, and having an awesome time.

It was a perfect way to end a period of my life that in many ways had stitched me back together after the darkness of St. Francis. I smiled over at her as she sat in the seat next to me, wearing a sparkly halter top and black skirt, along with the corsage I'd given her earlier. She grinned back silently yet knowingly. My heart skipped a beat.

Finally, we arrived at the dance and my dad parked the Jeep. We climbed out, and he clasped me on the shoulder before I got too far away from him, stopping me from leaving his sight for a moment.

"Have fun tonight Adam," he said. "Let me know when you guys are done. And remember; don't do anything I wouldn't do."

"Daaaadd," I groaned. He beamed proudly at me.

"Okay okay, you kids go have fun!" He nodded, chuckling as he climbed back into the Jeep and took off down the road. I looked over at Kara standing by the door and she beckoned me to join her inside.

§

I won't say that I'm a good dancer, but that night something came over me. I'm not sure if it was the fact that I was with someone I'd liked for much of the year, or the intoxication I felt knowing this was the end of an era (and I wouldn't see most of these people again). Whatever it was drew me out of my shell, if only a little. Kara somehow managed to make me just uncomfortable enough to step out and shake my butt. The problem was, being neurodivergent, I was really introverted and between the loud music and all the people present, I was feeling extremely overwhelmed. Initially, I was hesitant to get out on the dance floor at all.

"Come on Adam," Kara groaned, tugging my arm playfully. "I want to go dance."

"Alright, alright," I relented. A cold sweat formed at my collar. "But just so you know, I'm not very good at this."

"That's what everyone says! Come on — I know you well enough by now to know that you would secretly regret not joining me out there, no matter how nervous you are." She grinned.

She was right. I got to my feet and let Kara lead me to the dance floor, where she immediately took charge and jumped right in. Feeling galvanized, I soon joined in, shaking my butt, pumping my arms up and down, and wiggling my entire body awkwardly. I felt like a fish trying to escape a net.

"Yeah, shake it Adam." My classmate Nick stood a few feet away from me, dancing with his girlfriend and laughing at my performance. I was having so much fun the oncoming social anxiety was kept at bay. I think on some level I always knew I had it in me, but it always took a special type of person to bring it out.

As the night drew to a close, I found myself reflecting nostalgically on my high school experience. Sure, there were challenges, but overall I was blown away by how far I'd come. I felt confident, I had begun to find myself, and I felt ready for what came next.

No matter how nervous and uncertain I was about the path that lay ahead, I had chosen my fate. It was time to move on.

CHAPTER 17

There has always been a certain clichéd mystique to the freshman year in university. Many high school grads use it as an opportunity to stretch their wings for the first time. Still, there's also often a twinge of fear about all the change; worries as to whether you'll find your place. This was very much where I found myself in September of 2006, except as someone on the autistic spectrum, it was even more intense. Although I'd chosen this path the previous year and even grown to be excited about it as the summer dragged on, starting at Laurentian remained the single most daunting change in my life up to that point, and it weighed heavily on my mind when I arrived on campus for the first time. The school felt huge, I felt insignificant, and I was not prepared for that.

I don't belong here. I don't belong here. I REALLY DON'T BELONG HERE.

It rang through my mind as I sat in the Fraser Auditorium — a massive indoor amphitheatre packed to the gills with fellow first year students — for Intro to Computers and Applications. The echoing chorus was on repeat; an anxiety-fuelled kettle of vultures waiting to pick at my bones if, or when, I didn't make it. I felt lost in the horde — a feeling I'd not felt since my first day of high school. Except this time, I recognized no one.

It was worse than being the only member of Starfleet stranded on an alien world just due to the sheer size of

Laurentian University relative to anywhere I'd been before. Still, by that point I'd experienced this kind of thing a few times already, so I steadied myself and made my way to class.

And that's when I saw her.

She was five-foot-two, wearing a black tank top and jeans. On her head, a green army-style hat covered her dyed red hair and framed her glasses. I instantly liked her style — she reminded me of the crew I'd left behind at St. Bens, and seemed as overwhelmed by the whole university thing as I was. She stood quietly, glancing around occasionally as throngs of other students passed her by. I decided right then and there that she could probably use a friend and walked over.

"Hey," I said, my chest tight, words forced. "Is this Intro to the Twentieth Century?"

To my great relief, she smiled.

"I think it is. I'm glad I'm not the only one who was confused. I'm Briana." She stuck out a hand.

"Adam," I replied, my anxiety replaced by excitement. After all, she was cute, and friendly, and she was talking to me.

"Well Adam, it's good to meet a friendly face. I don't know anyone and it's all a little intimidating."

"Right?" I chuckled, still feeling a touch on edge.

"So, I guess you're into history too then?"

"I am," Briana beamed. "My dad never went to university, but he read a lot. Taught me a lot about history and stuff. It helps when I write my stories."

"You're a writer too?" I tried to keep things cool.

"Yeah, I write lots of spy-fi stuff. How about you?"

"Science fiction mainly," I said, "but I love spy stories too. I grew up watching James Bond movies."

"I love James Bond."

The conversation continued as the door opened and we made our way in, where we sat together at the back of the small auditorium.

We joked and made fun of the lecture a bit.

"Can you believe these seats?" I commented, squirming uncomfortably. Briana chuckled.

"I swear they think all students are right-handed. I call shenanigans!"

"Right?" I paused, her comment sinking in. "Wait — are you left-handed too?"

"Mhm," she nodded. "So, if you decide to make a stink about how hard it is to write on these little fold-out desk things as a leftie because they're made for righties ... I'd have your back."

"Oh God, I probably wouldn't bother," I said, face palming. "Is there any point?"

"You afraid?"

"What? Me? No, I ..."

Briana laughed and it was everything we could do to avoid drawing attention to ourselves. We became fast friends after that first day, spending time together on the days when our classes synced up and chatting constantly on MSN. She was my first university friend, but I also found myself thinking about more than that, and I wondered if she felt the same way.

Only time will tell, I remember thinking to myself as I went home after my first day at Laurentian. I still wasn't quite sure I belonged, but befriending Brianna had at least started to change that.

Maybe this university thing wouldn't be so bad after all.

§

Meeting Briana was the highpoint of my first day at Laurentian, but the very next day would come with challenges all its own. It was a sunny Tuesday in September, and the day had been exhausting. While Mondays and Wednesdays were short and only consisted of two classes in the afternoon (Computers and History), Tuesdays and Thursdays on the other hand, were a far more gruelling gauntlet of classes. In fact, they threatened to overwhelm me very easily because the irregular structure of alternating between early days and afternoons wreaked havoc on my sleep schedule. Like many autistics, I am a night owl by default, so having to go from staying up late to being in bed early every second day was really hard for me to do.

Needless to say, I was spent. I sat collapsed on the bench at the downtown bus terminal, eagerly waiting for my bus home to arrive while my backpack — heavy with my laptop and books — rested beside me. After a few minutes, and with rising boredom threatening to overcome me in that pre-smartphone era, I decided on a whim to pull my psychology textbook from my bag.

Opening the front cover, I revelled in the "new book smell"; that chemically sharp aroma born of a freshly produced, glossy-paged textbook. I'd always loved it, and I think the only smell that ever came close to eliciting the same reaction was it's opposite — musty, worn "old book smell." The pages were smooth and sleek to my touch, and I smiled. Here was a new book with so much to teach me.

I wonder what this book has to say about Asperger's? I thought, flipping to the index at the back and scanning for it. Sure enough, I soon found the word highlighted in bold, went to the listed page, and began reading. What I saw printed there threatened to sour the good mood the new book smell had put me in.

To say the textbook was less than kind (and accurate) regarding those on the autistic spectrum would be an understatement. Phrases like "may never develop normal relationships" and "severe communication and social issues" littered the page, echoing the words of Dr. Jackson all those years before. Eventually, it was all I could do to close the book and put it away, a simmering rage taking hold.

That can't be right, I thought to myself defensively, *this doesn't sound like me at all. Clearly, they got something wrong.*

I didn't realize it then, but I'd unwittingly stumbled across one of the biggest sore points among many autistic rights activists: the struggle between clinicians' view of the spectrum and the lived experiences of those who are actually on it.

While Asperger's as an official diagnostic label has since given way to Autism Spectrum Disorder in the newest edition of the Diagnostic and Statistical Manual of Mental Disorders, the tendency to classify autistic people according to many different function-related labels has remained. Terms like 'high functioning,' 'low functioning,' 'gifted,' 'severe,' 'quirky,' 'awkward,' and others continue to be used, which promote problematic and stereotypical views of autistics as obsessive, unemotional, 'savants', etc.. What I read that day in my textbook was a classic example of this.

Anyone reading the entry could be forgiven if they came away from the experience with a very limited understanding of people on the autism spectrum. After all, clinicians and parents' groups have long had the ability and power to shape the official autism narrative, along with the perspectives of mainstream society toward it, with autistic self-advocacy being a relatively young concept with less coverage and recognition in comparison.

Reading that chapter tapped into another sore spot, even if I didn't care to admit it — the feeling of being constantly underestimated. Ever since mom had first told me about Dr. Jackson's words, I'd felt shame and discomfort around the terms Asperger's and autism. It also didn't help that we didn't really talk about it very much at home except to ridicule Dr. Jackson for being off the mark. While I'm sure my parents did these things with the best of intentions, it combined with things like being asked if I wanted to use my IEP in high school to feel as though being anything other than normal was bad, and that I should be able to do everything everyone else could do just as easily because I was one of the 'smart' kids. I didn't want people to assume I was incapable just because of what I felt was an arbitrary label, and reading my psychology textbook that day did nothing to dispel my concerns that people would make such assumptions about me the moment I confided in them I was autistic. It was the same problem I'd had since the speech writing contest in middle school really; allowing myself to be vulnerable about this deep part of myself would inevitably lead to pain, so why should I bother?

Nope, I reasoned. *The book is wrong. It's got to be. There's way more to my life than that.*

§

The textbook's words may have soured me in the moment, but I quickly pushed them out of my mind. I had far more pressing concerns to think about — like whether or not Briana and I would get to date. I know how it sounds, but don't underestimate the power a new connection like this can have over an autistic person when we find ourselves in uncomfortable and unfamiliar situations. Laurentian University was an ocean compared to any school I'd been at before, and Briana represented a lifeline in my brain. I wasn't sure where we stood romantically, but I also knew that since I'd met her, I'd felt a little less anxious about the whole post-secondary ordeal. In many ways, she was my rock in those early days.

Evidently, Briana felt the same way about me because by the end of September, we'd admitted our feelings to each other. We'd spend hours together in the archives of the Laurentian library, cuddling and listening to music. We had deep emotional conversations down there and grew closer and closer by the day.

See? I thought to myself one night after class as we sat together. *There's no way that textbook or Dr. Jackson were right. If Asperger's means I can't read or understand people, how could I be doing all this with Briana?*

My younger self was both right and wrong about this. While it's true that the psychology textbook presented an overly simplified view of life on the spectrum and neglected to highlight the differences between the clinical perspective and lived experiences of autistic people, I also wasn't entirely on the same page as Briana in that moment. We each liked the other yes, but much like with Marie, I'd begun to go all-in emotionally with her. It was hard not to do — I'd not only grown-up autistic, but also in a Roman Catholic environment.

Strict, black and white rules around relationships and sex permeated my understanding of that aspect of myself, which further encouraged me to jump in and try to force a relationship to conform to the rigidity I'd been taught was morally pure. Briana may have liked me, but because of everything, I ended up expecting things to go a certain way. When the universe ultimately threw me a succession of curve balls, it threatened to upend my whole world.

§

It was Thanksgiving weekend, which translates to early October in Canada. My dad was still working as a teacher for the Sudbury Catholic District School Board at that point, so he and Trish were both out of the house every day. Since most first-year students had Fridays off, Briana and I planned to spend the day together at my place. It didn't take a rocket scientist to figure out what might be about to happen, and even as someone with an autistic brain, I'd heard more than enough stories from others to piece two and two together. Still, I was somewhat naïve. After all, if I really wanted things to stop — if, say, they got too heated or too intense for my comfort — I could easily stop right? I mean ... surely ... my head would remain clear?

Briana and I started off innocently enough: we were watching *House on Haunted Hill*, cuddled up on my double bed, kissing every so often when there was a lull in the action (in the movie, I mean). It wasn't long before this became more ... involved. Kissing led to heavier kissing, which led to petting, and eventually, before either of us realized what was going on, we were laying there with only our underwear to cover us as we fooled around. Up until that point, making out with Marie had been the extent of my intimate experiences. The afternoon I spent with Briana that fateful Friday in October involved far more than I'd ever done before. It challenged everything I'd been taught about sex, and shattered self-imposed boundaries and limitations I'd never realized I even had. I was shocked, I felt vulnerable, I'd never let my guard down so completely. We'd only been dating for three weeks by that point, and perhaps I'd latched on a little too quickly once everything was said and done, but in the moment (and with no prior experience to teach me otherwise) there was no doubt in my mind — I loved Briana with every fibre of my being.

Which is what made what happened next all the more painful.

Later that weekend, we'd just left my Zia and Zio's house after Thanksgiving dinner. There had been nine of us present — me, Ella, Amelia, Mark, Trish, and my dad, as well as my Zio, Zia, and Nona Olga — and it being an Italian meal, there was also no shortage of food. Between the antipasto dishes; the main course of turkey, stuffing, and spaghetti; and dessert (pumpkin pie, ice cream, and coffee of both the normal and "espresso" varieties), my stomach was bloated.

Thoughts of Briana swirled in my head as my dad drove us home. Once there, I flopped down on the couch in the basement, laptop on lap, and fired up MSN hoping to catch Briana for a quick chat. She had a friend named Matt from back home visiting for the weekend, and I was eager to find out how their visit went.

Awesome! She's online, I thought as I saw the little green MSN character beside her username.

ChaosMerdy: heyyy u! I miss u! How was ur weekend?

~Briana~: hey this is matt ... briana is just sleeping ill tell her u said hi!

ChaosMerdy: o no worries! Thx! Nice to meet u! How was ur day?

~Briana~: good! We slept together alot today lol. It was nice!

ChaosMerdy: haha ya i wish i could nap but i can't do it! Im jealous!

~Briana~: no dude i mean we had sex sorry haha i thought u knew!

My heart sank. The Tenth Doctor's voice rang through my head ("WHAAATT?") as my brain scrambled to make sense of the situation. *Did she ... cheat on me? For that matter, had we even discussed being exclusive?* It had never been explicitly stated but given how our relationship had gone up until that point, I assumed we were. My stomach turned as I considered I may have been wrong.

~**Briana**~: ya it was great! I liked her for a loooonngg time! Ur her friend Adam tho right? She says lots of amazing things about u man!

Clearly, I'd let myself get swept up in my own emotions and yet again misread a situation.

ChaosMerdy: thanks ... im glad u guys got to see each other 2day.

~**Briana**~: ya man! Was fun! Ur an awesome friend tho u know. She super appreciates u!

My stomach was in knots, and my mind was reeling, so Matt's words were cold comfort. I meant what I said to him, but I also felt like puking. I felt ridiculous and raw.

ChaosMerdy: well shes pretty cool too dude ... tell her i say hi! i need to get going tho. Good nite!

I hastily logged off then went to bed where I cried myself to sleep.

It shook me to my core, and I'd be lying if I said I quickly got over the pain of that moment. I couldn't believe how badly I'd misunderstood things, or how I'd allowed my feelings to get the better of me. I mean, looking back on it after a weekend of processing, it became quite clear to me that Briana and I had definitely been on different pages, and that I had jumped in too fast. I just couldn't help it — the situation was new, it overwhelmed all of my common sense and reason, and I got too emotionally invested too quickly because of it. It was just sex after all, and after a lifetime of internalizing repressive social dogma about it in the most black and white way imaginable (because yay, autistic thinking patterns), I finally came to understand exactly what people meant when they described the differences between physical and emotional intimacy.

Oh God, what if the textbook was right? I shuddered.

I felt raw, and when I saw Briana again on Wednesday, we each averted our gaze as we stood in the entrance hall of the Fraser building.

"Hey," I said at last, not knowing what else *to* say.

"Hey Adam," she replied, finally looking me in the eyes. "Listen ... I ..."

"What happened?" I blurted out. She sighed.

"Matt and I ... well I've known him for a long time. He's from back home. And as much as I'm here for school ..."

"... Sault Ste Marie is home," I sighed. "I get it."

"Yeah. I'm really sorry Adam. One thing led to another, and before either of us knew it..."

"Things got a lot more complicated than either of us wanted ... didn't they?"

"They really did," she replied, bowing her head. I furrowed my brow.

"I want you to know that I understand," I said at last. "We never really talked about what we were, if we were together officially, if we were exclusive — any of it. So, I get it. I'm not mad. But I do need some time to process this."

"I know," Briana said. "I know I hurt you, and I wish I could make things right ... but would you settle for a doughnut from Tim Hortons, and a game of *Donkey Kong Country* on your laptop while you process?"

I laughed in spite of myself. Almost as soon as we began hanging out between classes, I'd downloaded a Super Nintendo emulator for my laptop. Playing *Donkey Kong Country* co-operatively had rapidly become one of our shared traditions, and it warmed my heart that she offered it.

"I'd really like that."

"So ... friends?" She offered tentatively. I nodded.

"Friends."

§

Between the fury I felt over reading the Asperger's definition provided by my textbook, and my struggles with Briana, it's safe to say that my first year of university was rife with emotional difficulty and processing. It challenged my pre-conceptions of myself in every way imaginable — both when it came to relationships, and when it came to my understanding of my own brain. Meeting Briana dragged me out of my comfort zone and forced me to critically evaluate my attachment to all the beliefs I'd been raised with, along with the rigidity with which they'd been applied in my life. By the end of that year, I'd taken my first steps toward a more secular, liberal, sex-positive, and dare I say it — *feminist* — view of the world (though I didn't realize it at the time). For an autistic person who often felt more comfortable operating according to strictly defined social rules, this was huge. It was one of the first moments in my life where I realized that perhaps rules weren't as important as things like open, honest communication between people over feelings and boundaries. Had I been less beholden to the strictures of how I thought relationships *should* go and more open to actually asking Briana where she was at to ensure we were in agreement, things may have been a little easier on both of us.

But I digress. I was definitely more rigid-minded than I would have cared to admit back then, and in that way, maybe the textbook definition that enraged me so wasn't entirely off the mark. What it lacked was something I've mentioned many times here before — nuance. Autistic people really *do* struggle with change and navigating social situations, and these are definitely aspects of my first year at LU that I found difficult. Then as now though, I refused to accept what the book had to say about me. It didn't feel complete, or authentic to my own experiences. I knew there had to be more to the story.

Little did I know, opportunities would soon present themselves for me to learn exactly what more looked like.

CHAPTER 18

Ten pages. Ten whole pages.

My blood ran cold at the mere thought. Dr. Larson — our professor for Intro to the 20th Century, and a physically imposing man who sported a shaved head and long, thick beard — had just given us our first major assignment for the class. I was petrified. In high school, I'd only ever written a maximum of five pages for any given project, and even that sometimes felt like pulling teeth. Ten pages was too much, and I shuddered at the mere thought.

That first essay was a mess of complex emotions. I felt overwhelmed by the workload and had no idea where to even start. This is a common problem among those of us who are autistic, have ADHD, or both. Often, executive dysfunction rears its ugly head, and we find ourselves paralyzed. It's as though the task is a tall brick wall standing in your way. Logically, you know that there are ways you could either break through or otherwise bypass it, but when you stand back and look at it, all you see is the wall stretching for miles in either direction.

The prominent neurodivergent youtuber Jessica McCabe has spoken before about the so-called 'wall of awful' on her channel *How to ADHD*, and I mention it here because it's extremely appropriate. Larson's essay assignment was absolutely a wall of awful. One of the tallest, longest, and scariest I'd seen in my entire educational career up to that point. The problem was, I had no choice but to try and scale it as best I could. The essay needed to be done, and no amount of fear on my part would change that.

Knowing we both felt similarly, Briana suggested that we meet up at the library after class and attempt to hammer out at least some progress on it. We'd been broken up for a few weeks by that point, but our newfound attempt at friendship was proving successful, and we discovered that we actually worked quite well together as an academic team. In light of that, I agreed and that night, we sat across from each other by one of the library's big bay windows, laptops out, and tried to get something written.

I felt the warm rays of sunset shining in through the window as I tried to focus on my laptop screen. Every time I went to type something on the keyboard though, my brain hit a mental wall. It was the same one I'd hit since I was a kid struggling to do my homework immediately after school according to Trish's rules. I knew I had to accomplish something, but my chest grew heavy, and heart pounded hard every time I thought about it. It was almost physically painful to even try. Because of this, I found myself staring out the window, transfixed by the red glow in the air as day transitioned to night.

Sunsets are so beautiful, I thought to myself. Then I snapped out of it.

No. I need to focus.

Forcing my gaze down to my screen, I began to type and managed to write a good page or so before calling it quits for the day. It was hard though, with each word I typed feeling like I was smashing my head against the invisible brick wall, and I found myself constantly fighting to keep on task. Briana had become similarly frustrated, and we decided to meet up again later that week to continue our hard work. Packing up my laptop and books, I made my way home for the night.

The biggest problem that presented itself as I hammered away at that assignment was my attention span ... or lack thereof. There were moments where it felt like I was on a decrepit wooden roller coaster that was rapidly running out of track. My mind would wander constantly, and while allowing my brain to drift slightly by browsing the internet in class was a good strategy because it allowed me a break from having to pay attention, I had to be careful lest I not pay attention at all, or worse — get sucked so deeply into hyperfocus land that I forgot I had an assignment to do to begin with. When it came to writing things like that first research paper, I could not keep my focus on the project for too long before I lost interest. This would often happen almost as soon as I opened Microsoft Word, though with some practice I was able to keep myself going long enough to finish a paragraph or two, maybe a page. Executive dysfunction is a bitch, and it was an internal battle I still faced, even years after my homework wars with Trish as a kid.

Even still, I didn't like the thought of asking for help at first. After all, I was one of the smart kids, and even though I'd done it once before out of sheer necessity, I wasn't quite ready to do it again. I mean, that was for math. I knew I sucked at math. But this — this was History. Writing. Language. They were my three preferred flavours of academic jam, and as far as I was concerned, I shouldn't need any help doing well in them. Hardship be damned — I would Hulk smash through that essay because I had no other choice.

Stubbornness was clearly never a trait I found myself lacking in.

I struggled with writing my essay for weeks before I finally brought it up to Mitch one night in a moment of frustration not unlike Captain Kirk's infamous "KHAAAAAAANN!" shout in *Star Trek II*.

"I don't know how everyone else does it. I feel overwhelmed."

"I know what you mean," Mitch said sympathetically.

"But I have a trick for you that's gotten me out of a few nasty assignments."

"I'm all ears," I exclaimed. Mitch nodded.

"You need to break it up into manageable chunks," he explained. "Whenever I do a big essay like that, I do one page per day, and then leave it at that. If you start early enough, you can get it done and not get overwhelmed."

My jaw dropped at the simple brilliance of his suggestion. I had honestly never thought about doing it that way before. It just sounded so easy when he put it that way.

"Does that work?" I asked, cocking an eyebrow skeptically.

"It sure does. At least for me. How do you think *I* got through first year?"

I nodded as I processed this. Mitch was a year older than me and was already well into his second year at Laurentian. Maybe there was something to his idea after all. I just didn't like that I felt as though I needed to do things differently than others. It made me self-conscious, even though I knew it shouldn't. Truthfully, it also seemed a little like changing a video game's difficulty setting to 'easy' mode. You could totally do it ... and no one would know or try to stop you ... but there existed a stigma around doing it all the same. *Real* gamers didn't need to after all ... or so people claimed. Even still, I *had* done it once before in Grade 11 ... and it wasn't as though I was asking for any official accommodations with the subject matter in this case — I was *more* than capable of writing and communicating well — it was just an adjustment to my own internal schedule. Did that even qualify as changing the difficulty setting?

I decided it didn't, so I went home after talking to Mitch and got to work on my paper. It was due in under a month, and with Mitch's help I had laid out my plan: for the next ten days, I'd write one page per day. After that, I'd give myself a few days to edit and cite my sources. If all went according to plan, I'd actually get it done early. If not? Those extra days could serve as a buffer zone in case I had a hard time getting anything done on any particular day.

It worked. I got a 75% grade on that first essay, and it felt amazing. It wouldn't, however, be the only time that I'd come face to face with my concentration and time management difficulties during my university career. Even though a planned-out schedule like this worked for me in terms of getting assignments done, I found entirely new struggles awaited me once I reached the end of my program and started Teacher's College.

Despite generally loving my undergraduate years, my sense of uncertainty with the teaching decision never did disappear. It persisted throughout most of my university career, though by the time I got to Teacher's College (a.k.a. "Pro Year"), I had at least come to a realization about myself; I wanted to help people and make the world a better place. I'd always had a political and activist bent, along with a stubborn need for fairness, and it had informed everything in my life from my earliest confrontations with Kay, to the speech writing competition in middle school and beyond. As such, it was only fitting to me that whatever I chose to do with my life should incorporate that desire. Over the course of several placements I'd had to do by that point, I'd decided that teaching would in fact be a pretty great way to achieve this goal, so I went into the final year of my program with cautious enthusiasm for the path I'd found myself on.

It didn't last. And not because of the subject matter.

Every day of Teacher's College felt like barely managed overwhelm for me. We had so many assignments I could hardly keep up, and I even embarrassingly forgot about one entirely until the day it was due. I was floundering, and I just wanted to throw my metaphorical controller at the TV and rage quit. The difficulty was set too high.

The judgmental glare of my classmates and teacher convinced me that something had to give though, and so I reached a decision; using an essay writing schedule for myself throughout undergrad *did* in fact retroactively count as lowering the difficulty to 'easy mode,' and I was going to do it all over again now. I downloaded a personal organizer app from the Mac App Store and used it to track all of my classes and assignments down to the letter. I didn't do this with the conscious thought that I was accounting for my spectrum-dwelling brain's strengths and weaknesses — I just wanted to survive the year and not fail — but that was exactly what my strategy did. My laptop (by that point a sleek-yet-aging 2008 aluminum MacBook) became an extension of my brain, and in a very real way it acted like a memory card for the game save files my brain just didn't have the internal storage capacity to hold anymore.

It was, in short, a revelation.

By offloading my organization and time management tasks to my laptop, I felt able to breathe again. It made me think back to that fateful day in Grade 11 when I finally decided to accept accommodations and write my exam in the special room. Except this time, it felt even more empowering.

I didn't realize it then, and I wouldn't come to be officially co-diagnosed with ADHD until almost a decade later, but by the end of teacher's college, I'd fought a year-long battle against the worst of my ADHD traits. Best of all — I'd found strategies that worked for me and won my own way. Because of this, a year later, when I did my Master's in History as I'd always wanted to, I wasn't ashamed of pursuing accommodations more officially through Laurentian's accessibility office. Even if it was just to get a new computer when the time came. Tech was my accommodation — that much had become clear to me.

My brain definitely doesn't work like everyone else's, I remember admitting to myself at last sometime in January of teacher's college — itself no small victory. We happened to be talking about autism and ADHD in class that day, which may have helped. During the lecture, my professor's words brought me back to that sunny Tuesday in September of 2006 when I had first read the clinical definition of Asperger's. I both scowled and chuckled to myself as I remembered the rage I felt that day. It turned out I had been right — autism was a far more complex and nuanced thing than that book managed to communicate. I still didn't know the half of it, but I started to reflect on my own life experiences and how they compared. The truth was, I *had* struggled socially, and relating to others did tend to be more difficult than it had to be at times. And then there were all the times I had to seemingly fight harder than my classmates to accomplish the same goals because I just wasn't interested enough in the subject matter to care. But there was also this whole other side to being autistic that wasn't captured by clinicians. There was the passion, the hyperfocus, and the ability to sink into the things that *did* engage me. Our professor seemed to understand that, and I immediately found myself absorbed in what she had to say.

As I was sitting there paying attention though, I noticed an undergrad student walk by the open door to our classroom. They stopped for a few minutes and listened to the lecture, then rolled their eyes as our professor explained autism in more detail, proclaiming silently yet quite effectively that they felt the whole lesson was a waste of time before continuing down the hall. I groaned, feeling personally attacked yet not willing to call attention to myself over some random student. The eye roll moment did however have another effect; it stirred a stubborn determination to defend myself that I'd not felt since middle school.

There's nothing at all wrong with being autistic, I thought to myself, scowling. *Maybe it's time for me to embrace my difference after all.*

... or at least, start to. Baby steps, right?

CHAPTER 19

"No, Luke; *I* am your father!"

Darth Vader's confrontation with young Skywalker in Cloud City will forever be burned into my mind. I'm always on the edge of my seat, every time I watch that scene in *The Empire Strikes Back*. It's my favourite *Star Wars* movie by far, and the moment in question has gone down in cinema history as truly iconic. When I think back on it though, it's also a turning point; the moment when Luke goes from simply reacting to events around him to embracing his own destiny and exerting his own will. Or at least trying to. He *did* ultimately play right into Darth Vader's hands because of it. But you know, details.

I also had such a moment, in February of 2011.

We were in the home stretch of pro year; only three months until our final placements and four months until we were done. The year had been overwhelming, and I longed for it all to be over. Before we reached the end though, we had several final projects to turn in, and one of them in particular meant a great deal to me personally. One of our professors had tasked us to present on an important education-related topic of our choosing. It could be whatever we wanted, but it had to be a multimedia presentation. I immediately knew I wanted to present on Asperger's Syndrome.

I know, I know — history repeats itself. But between reading about the clinical definition of Asperger's in first year and coming face to face with my own executive functioning difficulties academically, events throughout university up to that point had convinced me that it was necessary to step out of my comfort zone and try to self-advocate again. At least, a little bit. I wasn't quite ready to come out of the neurodivergent closet or anything — I was far too worried about people judging me entirely on the basis of my diagnosis instead of on my worth as a human being. But it was becoming blatantly obvious to me after chewing on the differences between the clinical diagnosis and my own life experiences for four years that perhaps being on the spectrum was some form of politicized identity after all. Maybe it was something more people needed to learn about from the perspective of someone who actually lived it.

I'm getting a bit ahead of myself though. First of all, I want to take you back to my fourth year of university at Laurentian. By that point, I'd pushed the textbook definition out of my mind and focused squarely on getting through my coursework. I always knew autism was part of my world, but I didn't give it any serious thought other than the aforementioned battles with executive dysfunction. Arguably, between all my classes and the feelings of overwhelm that came with them, I had far more pressing things on the brain. I was Luke Skywalker on Tatooine, more preoccupied with the work his Uncle Owen had given him than with the secret mission R2-D2 claimed to be on.

Things got a bit more interesting when I started taking Dr. Landry's Issues in Catholic Education course as part of my program. In that class, I met my friend Emily — a queer fellow sci-fi geek with a social conscience and a love of learning. We hit it off almost immediately on the bus home one night after class.

"Um, hi," I began awkwardly. Emily looked over at me and immediately averted her gaze.

"Hi ..."

"I just wanted to say that your point about LGBT issues in class was really good," I began, struggling to propel the conversation onward. "You seemed really cool, and I wanted to chat more. I hope that's okay?"

"Oh, it's fine," she replied. "It's Adam, right?"

"Yep. Emily?"

"Mhm," she said. "What are you taking?"

"History," I replied. "But I've taken a lot of anthropology classes, too."

"I love cultural anthropology," she said, perking up at the anthropology reference.

"I took it in first year," I said enthusiastically. "I love the whole concept that social mores are culturally relative."

"Exactly. Almost makes you think of the Prime Directive ..."

"You're a Trekkie, too?"

Our conversation continued along these lines for the rest of the bus ride, until we both finally reached our respective homes. I was smitten; a feeling which was to be short lived because before long, Emily picked up on my infatuation and subtly let slip that she wasn't interested. While I was a bit disappointed at first, we quickly grew very close, and I came to think of her as my sister in a lot of ways.

Something that quickly became a tradition for us was to meet up before class and go for dinner on Wednesday nights. Where we went would vary by the week, but being two starving students, the typical choices were Tim Hortons and Pita Pit (though sometimes we'd go to our favourite Mexican place downtown, Casa Mexicana). One Wednesday in particular, we found ourselves sitting at Pita Pit, hastily scarfing down some pitas (chicken caesar with bacon and croutons in my case). Over the course of our dinner conversation, we somehow landed on the topic of gender equality.

"I don't know if I believe in feminism," I explained. "It should be about equality, shouldn't it? Men and women and other genders, all being given equal opportunities."

Emily giggled. I asked her why and she grinned.

"Um, Adam? That makes you a feminist. That's exactly it. Equality."

"What? No ... but how?"

"You're probably coming at this based on growing up male

and only really getting the media stereotypes around feminism," she expounded, "but it really is all about equality. Think about it this way; when someone calls the fire department because their house is on fire, you wouldn't expect them to douse every house on the street with water, right? Like, they'd focus on the one that's actually burning down?"

"Well obviously," I replied. She nodded and continued.

"Well feminism is the same way — it tries to achieve equality by focusing on a specific area of inequality and making it better. In this case, it's how women have been oppressed by society, but it's really the same with any activist group. You achieve equality by targeting the inequalities and working to fix them. Know what I mean?"

I was flabbergasted. I opened my mouth to respond, but somewhere in the few seconds between her uttering the word "feminist" and my attempt to reply, my brain began processing everything.

"I just ... have never thought of it that way before."

"Well, that's what you have me around for now, isn't it?" She tilted her head as she took a bite out of her pita, brushing a lock of brown hair out of the way.

"Not the *only* reason you know ..."

"Oh, how could I forget? Commander Sovak and Captain Marin are a team, aren't they?"

I chuckled as I thought about the *Star Trek* role-play Emily and I had casually started one evening after class. My character was the half-Vulcan, half-human Commander Sovak, while she was Captain Inari Marin, a joined Trill.

"Well, I mean it is the responsibility of the First Officer to make sure his captain doesn't do anything too reckless on an away mission."

"True ... Captain Marin does have a wild streak. Not all of her past lives were quite as duty bound."

"Sovak is quite aware of that," I acknowledged, before adding. "But you're the captain — I defer to your judgment."

"Smart man," Emily grinned. "Especially after what we just

talked about." We laughed and packed up our things. If we lingered any longer, we'd be late for class, so we made a mad dash to the bus terminal across the street.

That one simple conversation had a huge impact on me. For so long, I'd felt as though I had this dark secret that needed hiding; one that differentiated me somehow, and made others think I was *broken* unless I proved them wrong first. As such, I had learned to be *very* careful about who I confided in about being on the spectrum. Learning about feminism was the point where that began to change. After all, if feminism could fight for equality by advancing the cause of one group in particular, surely that could apply to all manner of other groups too, right? It led me directly to a related philosophy; "the self is political." It was the idea that everything we are was impacted by and could impact politics. And that identities could and should be cherished, defended, and uplifted instead of suppressed in the name of conformity. Identities like having Asperger's, being autistic, or however else you wanted to word it.

This combined with another concept I quickly discovered as, newly inspired, I clicked further down the internet rabbit hole — neurodiversity. It literally meant 'diversity of human minds.' A neurodiversity perspective on psychology would argue that much like humans are diverse in literally every other way, we're diverse when it comes to our minds too. It argues there is no "normal" human mind, and things like autism, ADHD, and schizophrenia are part of the normal range of variation that exists in humanity.

After over a decade of feeling the opposite, my jaw dropped. I couldn't believe it!

The more I read about this, the more excited I felt. It went beyond learning how to cope with and manage being autistic — I'd done that for a lifetime already. Coping and managing weren't enough anymore, and I grew to feel they were distasteful and pathologizing ways of viewing what I increasingly saw as my natural wiring. Finding neurodiversity was when I realized I was perfectly okay the way I was. It was the moment I stopped running from the diagnosis Dr. Jackson had seen fit to bestow on me 14 years before and instead turned to face it. I wasn't sure if I was quite ready to embrace it just yet, but I was ready to stop being afraid of it. And for me, that was huge.

Which is why when Jan Barclay gave us the multimedia assignment at the end of pro year, I knew I had to do it about Asperger's. It was my *Empire Strikes Back* moment; the point where I stopped letting fate pull me along and instead took the metaphorical bull by the horns. I very obviously *did* have a politicized identity, and it was high time I scored a decisive victory in its defense. Emily even helped me find the perfect song for the slide show I'd opted to put together for the project; *Why Don't You Let Me Stay Here?* by She and Him. It was quirky, upbeat, and fun, which was perfect for the positive spin I was trying to put on my project. *After all,* I reasoned, *there are far too many negative messages out there about autism — I want to do something different.*

"I think it's great for your presentation," Emily smiled as we sat in her bedroom in the student house she shared with several other roommates. It was an old wood-panelled home with lots of character. I nodded excitedly.

"I do too," I replied. "But I'm really nervous; I haven't been this open about any of this in a long time. What if people judge me afterward?"

"They might," Emily said. She was sitting cross-legged on her bed looking at me as I sat at her desk, laptop out and open with my work-in-progress on the screen.

"But that's their problem, not yours. And besides, you aren't actually saying *you* are autistic in it — only presenting about it as a topic."

"You're right," I agreed. "Plus they probably already suspect something's weird about me." Emily giggled as I said that.

"Adam you *are* weird. But that's not a bad thing at all. The best people in this world are weird, and honestly, I wouldn't be your friend if you weren't. Normies are so ... boring ..."

I grinned as she said this, feeling less nervous about my

project as we spoke. Emily was right — I was ready. I was going to do it. And no one was going to stand in my way.

§

It was a cold day in February 2011. I stood at the front of our small class of 20, fiddling with my MacBook as I struggled to get it hooked up to the room's AV system. This was it — the day had come. It was time to present my multimedia project about Autism Spectrum Disorder (because by then, the DSMV was only two years away and terminology had already changed to reflect the shift away from Asperger's). My hands were shaking as I made the final calibrations and verified that my screen was outputting on the class Smartboard. I was as ready as I'd ever be, and the class was looking to me with interest.

I knew from experience not all of them really knew what autism was. Some were operating on outdated assumptions, and others had never truly given it any serious thought. I hoped to at least begin to change that that day. After quieting down the residual chatter a bit, Jan motioned for me to begin. I nodded to her at the back of the class, my finger hovering nervously over the spacebar for several seconds before finally pressing it. I took a deep breath to calm myself, then sat down as my multimedia presentation unfolded to the chipper tune of She and Him's song.

"Adam that was wonderful," our professor praised from the back of the room ten minutes later as my video came to an end. She clapped a few times in approval as she spoke. I smiled in spite of myself as I stood back up.

"Does anyone have any questions for Adam?"

At that point, several hands shot up and a surge of anxiety shot down my spine.

Oh God, this is going to be the speech competition all over again, isn't it? I took another deep breath and steeled myself before looking over at the first of my classmates to raise his hand, a tall bald man by the name of Ralph.

"Yeah, your presentation was awesome Adam just wanted to say that. But I was wondering ... what made you choose this topic in particular?"

I did everything I could to keep myself centred as I processed his question. Putting my hands in the pockets of my zip-up hoodie, I forced a smile.

"Thanks Ralph. Let's just say I have some personal experience with all of this."

Ralph nodded in approval and I sat down after answering a few more questions from my classmates. Eventually, Jan moved on to the next presenter, but I couldn't help but feel as though things had changed for me in that brief moment. The journey that had begun all those years ago in elementary school had reached a turning point much like Luke's had in the middle installment of the Original Trilogy.

They say the Force speaks to those who listen. I'd spent much of my life running from it, but that day, for the first time, I stopped and listened to what it had to say. I felt like a Jedi Padawan learner who had just faced his darkest fear and finally allowed the Force to fill his entire being. I knew I could never go back to how things had been before. I could never again be afraid of being on the autistic spectrum. The textbook was wrong after all — being autistic wasn't a deficit; it was beautiful, normal, and oh-so human. I'd embraced neurodiversity, or at least started to.

The trial was complete, and for better or worse, I was a changed person.

CHAPTER 20

Embracing my authentic self was one thing but proclaiming it to the world was another matter entirely. I knew as early as 2012 I wanted to use my story to help others along the path to self-knowledge and self-acceptance — my experiences thus far had taught me that much — but I was still very anxiety-ridden about the whole thing. I mean, how could I not be when most people I confided in about being autistic started looking at me differently almost immediately after I'd told them? In light of that, I decided to do what seemed sensible; I'd Google search other autistic self-advocates and see if there were any others out there doing what I wanted to do. Perhaps that would give me some idea of how to proceed.

I didn't find many, but the one blog I did stumble across became very important to me. It was called *Asperger's Illustrated* and it was written by an autistic blogger and advocate named Steph, who lived in New York City. I smiled to myself as I scrolled down the front page of her blog — she drew video game characters and was a very talented artist, which made me really happy. I found myself relating both to her ramblings about daily life as a spectrum dweller, and about school, interests, everything. She was really cool, and as I read more of her posts, I came to feel as though I'd come home. I'd found a kindred spirit. Someone else out there got it. Someone else out there had similar experiences with autism to my own and saw fit to share her story with the world.

If Steph could do it, so could I.

Somehow, this fellow autistic, geeky human from one of the largest cities in the world who I had never met or even spoken to had inspired me and shown me that what I wanted to do could be done. I was galvanized. I was motivated. I set up a simple new blog in a flurry of productivity using the free Blogger platform and was ready to get started.

... But I still needed a topic for my first post.

I wracked my brain for some time, trying to figure out exactly what to write about. I wanted to use my platform to educate about autism from the perspective of lived experience, while also helping my autistic readers realize they too were not alone. Determining what to say on that front was harder than it should have been though. I wrote a few generic posts explaining what I hoped to accomplish, but it wasn't long before I put the project aside for the time being. I was in the home stretch of my Master's degree, and the year had proven to yet again be filled with overwhelm. I needed to get through it, finish my thesis, and be done with school for good. Around June though, inspiration hit.

I woke up one lazy Saturday morning feeling thoroughly stressed about the thesis work I had ahead of me that day and decided to browse the internet while my brain booted up. I'd been idly reading through blogs about bullying while thinking about my own experiences with it, when one of them proudly proclaimed Taylor Swift's new song *Mean* to be the anthem of the anti-bullying movement.

My ears perked up, and I decided to give it a listen. I was skeptical — I'd never really given Taylor Swift much of a chance before that, but what I heard of her message through the catchy, lively tune stuck with me. It instantly became one of my favourite songs. More importantly though, it also made me realize exactly what my topic needed to be, bullying.

Even ten years later, my memories of middle school still hurt to think about. I had locked them away deep in my brain;

accessible if desired, but not often brought back up because to do so was painful enough. To do so willingly, after all that time, was scary to me. It was also something I knew needed to be done, especially now that I'd begun accepting and embracing my autistic brain. Besides, the advantage of a blog was, even if I wasn't fully comfortable being out in the open, I didn't have to in any way associate it with Facebook. I could even use a few pen names — Adam Michael and Mike Laurence (my middle name) — in order to keep things private enough to be comfortable for me. It felt like the perfect balance between getting my story out there, and self-preservation. I even had a topic now.

With that in mind, I set to work. It was very hard to write, but weirdly enough, I started to feel lighter than I ever had as I did so. Facing all of that grief and anguish and pain again after so long was very much like that moment in *The Empire Strikes Back* when Luke faced the apparition of Darth Vader in the cave on Dagobah, only to realize what he was truly afraid of was the darkness inside himself.

I had a lot of *Empire Strikes Back* moments apparently (I did mention it's my favourite Star Wars movie, didn't I?), but that was what I was facing; my own darkness, a side of my soul and psyche that I had kept safely tucked away for a decade while I grew and developed from broken boy to well-adjusted man. That broken boy had never truly gone away though — he only sat back and watched as life passed him by and progressed ever forward. My post for my blog was the beginning of healing for him, and I felt overcome by happiness and peace as I realized this.

It was time for young 13-year-old Adam to finally get his closure. Or at least start to. And if it also helped spark a conversation about autism in the process? Bonus. With newfound determination, I set to work.

The effect of all this oppression and misery at the hands of my classmates is that my young 13/14 year old self was taken mentally and emotionally to the darkest place I can safely say I've been in my entire life, I wrote, heart pounding in my chest as I expressed a painful truth for the first time ever. After keeping at it for what felt like hours, I'd managed to pump out the equivalent of a small essay on my experiences at St. Francis. My soul was raw, my eyes were bloodshot from staring at a computer screen, and my hands begged me to be done with all the work. Before I could call it a night though, I had one more thought to get out. I stretched my fingers, and put them to the keyboard once more, feeling a complex mix of sadness and joy as I did.

Even in the darkest of the darkness, however, I typed, pushing back against a torrent of tears, *there was always a speck of light in my life. The kindness of my friends, the love of my family, and the constant hope that things would get better; these are the things that sustained me and pulled me back from this place and helped me through those years. Things did eventually get better.*

I stared at that final sentence for several minutes, processing the deep emotional catharsis it represented. My mind was so flooded by feeling in that moment that I found myself unable to speak for a long time after finishing my piece. It's been said that autistic people can often lose the ability to speak verbally when confronted with intense emotions, and that was definitely what I was going through. Finally, I managed to take a deep gasp of air and exhaled, pushing with it all the negativity, anger, and sadness I'd held onto from those years.

It was done.

Satisfied that I'd written everything that needed writing, I checked for any obvious grammatical mistakes, formatted it, and clicked the big "Post" icon at the top of the page.

And that was that. I had put a deeply personal story from my past on the internet for all to see. Terrified didn't even begin to describe how I felt. But I was also proud, and grinning ear to ear.

I had done it! To quote Obi-Wan Kenobi, I'd taken my first step into a wider world.

§

What surprised me most about the aftermath of my first few posts was just how much traction they gained. At first, writing and posting felt like screaming into the void of the internet. It was as though I was the SETI project, sending communication signals out into the cosmos, looking desperately for alien life yet feeling as though no one was truly listening. Except in my case, it turned out people were.

My first four posts didn't receive a huge amount of views, but I was amazed by just how many they did get, including many from all over the world. My jaw dropped as I saw this and realized there was no way the viewership was limited to simply those who knew me. It was enough to convince me to keep going, and so I did. After a brief work-related hiatus (I had just graduated from school and started working, so the blog fell by the wayside while I sorted life out), I got myself into a routine of writing a new article every two weeks for it. I even updated the look and feel of my page from the simple and basic quick one I had chosen when I first started to something sleeker and more modern. As I did, I noticed the view numbers had expanded even more. There were now people reading my writing from all over the globe and logging in from a variety of web browsers on a plethora of platforms. It wasn't enough to propel me to celebrity status in the online world, but it was a comfortable little following.

As it turned out, the void was staring back, and it made my heart happy that my writing had reached some people out there too. I had always wanted to be a writer after all, I just never thought this was how I would do it. Video game and movie reviews? Sure. Science fiction stories? Absolutely. But sharing deeply personal anecdotes about my life hadn't been my first thought. Even so, it was hard to argue with the results — especially if my work was helping people. Which, of course, was the other thing I had always wanted to do. I still wasn't ready to attach my real name to this little project, nor was I ready to tie it in with Facebook and be more out than I was at that time (I was still keeping my spectrum-dwelling status on a "close friend and family" basis in the real world because of my experiences in the past), but that original blog was the start of something for me. I had begun wading into the ocean of online autistic self-advocacy. Even if I was only ready to have my feet in the water? It was still way further in than I'd ever been before. It was more than I long thought I'd ever be willing or able to do.

And you know what? It felt pretty damn good.

CHAPTER 21

"By the right of the Council, by the will of the Force, I dub thee Jedi; knight of the Republic."

These were the words spoken to Kanan Jarrus during the ancient and sacred ritual that was the Jedi knighting ceremony in an episode of *Star Wars Rebels* in 2016. In the show, it was a long overdue moment for Kanan — a character who had never officially been knighted but who had stepped up to fight the Empire all the same — and I remember being thrilled to finally see it happen on screen. It was by this simple phrase that a Padawan achieved the rank of Jedi Knight and completed their training. But there was one important trial that remained before this could happen; the Padawan had to construct their own lightsaber. The lightsaber was after all a symbol of the Jedi path as a whole and represented both the achievements of the Jedi in question, and their voice in the world. It also represented their commitment to standing up, speaking out, and defending the innocent.

In 2015, I built my own lightsaber. Metaphorically, of course.

My friend Maggie and I had developed a tradition by that point of going for car rides and talking about everything under the sun. She was a new friend I'd made since graduating and entering the workforce, and she'd rapidly become one of my favourite people. We'd met through our mutual friend Kelli, who I had encountered because we both worked at the mall. We both loved the car ride concept as a hangout because it allowed us to talk without having to feel weird about not wanting to make eye contact.

Yeah, she got me.

That night in particular, we had been talking about my blog and the writing I'd been doing for it when a thought came to her.

"Have you ever considered starting a Facebook page for this stuff Adam?"

I was dumbfounded and also very nervous. I'd shied away from that for a long time because of wanting to maintain at least some privacy around my diagnosis. I had accepted myself as being autistic yes, but I didn't necessarily want to proclaim it on my personal Facebook either. I wasn't sure I wanted to go that far, and I told Maggie as much.

"I just ... I don't want to make those two worlds cross, you know? I kinda have some privacy right now and I like it this way."

"I get that, dude, I really do," she replied, going quiet for a few seconds as she executed a turn onto a side street in Sudbury's Minnow Lake area. "But just think of how many people you could reach if you did that. I mean, didn't you tell me the whole reason you kept going with the teaching program despite being unsure was because you wanted to help people?"

"Yeah ... I suppose," I considered out loud, acknowledging she was right as I sipped from my coffee. "But I don't know ... I have lots of people on Facebook who don't know, and even more who I don't necessarily *want* to know. It's kind of a big risk."

"Sure, but what's the worst any of them could say or do about it?"

"They could think differently of me and act weird."

"So?" Maggie slowed the car to a stop as we reached a red light and looked over at me.

"Does any of that really matter? There are also laws that

exist that would stop your workplace from discriminating against you for any of this. So why not be more open?"

"Honestly? I'm scared." The words came out of my mouth before I could stop them, so I continued the train of thought. "It's taken me this long to just be this comfortable with myself, and I like where I'm at. But I know being fully open and out about being autistic would invite discrimination and I don't think I want to deal with that."

Maggie sighed, and I knew she was about to dispense some tough love.

"Dude, come on! Just look how far you've come already. You're way WAY stronger than you give yourself credit for."

"I guess ..."

"Don't guess — know. Know it. Because it's true. You're a goddamn warrior Adam; I don't see you doing what you're doing now for the rest of your life. I never have. I see you making a living doing this kind of thing. Writing about autism, speaking out, talking about it and educating others. I seriously think that's your destiny, dude, not working at the mall wasting away. Not that there's anything wrong with any kind of workplace because capitalism shits on all of us and fuck it. But you know what I mean ... "

"Absolutely. Fuck capitalism," I replied, grinning. I thought about what Maggie had just said, and her words struck me. Not the capitalism bit, though that was certainly true; no, the part about my destiny. In an instant, I relived my experiences speaking out about autism in both middle school and university and realized I had always been drawn to doing just that. I had always been scared too, but it had never stopped me from wanting to speak out. It felt like being in acting class all over again giving my performance of *The Jabberwocky*. I was terrified then as well, but doing the thing anyway had been empowering. Maggie was right — I *was* a warrior.

Maybe this would be the same.

"You might be right," I responded at last. "You really think all that?" Maggie groaned.

"Adam, when will you realize that I don't say *anything* unless it's true? I mean come on; you know me by now. Blunt honesty and all that."

"It's true — have I ever told you how much I love that about you?"

"Frequently," she chuckled, "but please don't stop. Yes Adam, I do think all that. And given how many people are on Facebook, I think a page may be perfect. Plus, you can still keep things separate to some degree. I just think once you do this, you won't want to anymore."

"Maybe you're right," I repeated, smiling as I finished my coffee. It was good timing too — Maggie had just pulled up in front of the apartment building I was living in with Mitch as my roommate.

"I know I am. In fact, I think you should go start a Facebook page tonight, while this conversation is fresh in your mind."

"I think I might."

"Not might — will. I'll be checking dude! And I believe in you."

"Thanks Maggie," I said, climbing out of the car and nodding at her. She waved goodnight and drove off into the distance as I walked inside and rode the elevator to my unit.

"Back already?" Mitch was laying on the couch watching TV, and looked over at the door as I came in.

"Yeah, Maggie couldn't be super late because she works tomorrow," I replied. I took off my jacket and boots and put them away, then made my way into the apartment proper.

"And how is Maggie?" he asked, grinning. "You know I've always liked her. She tells it like it is."

"Yeah, well she definitely had some interesting things to tell tonight that's for sure."

"Oh?" Mitch sat up on the couch and peered over at me intently as I sat in the armchair across from him in our living room.

"Maggie thinks I should start a Facebook page for my

autism blog," I informed him, hoping for his input on the matter. Mitch thought about this for a few moments.

"Well, why don't you? I'm kinda surprised you haven't already to be honest."

"Really?"

"Yeah. I mean it's the logical next step, isn't it? It would grow your follower base."

"But it would also mean being more out about this than I've ever been before. On my blog I use a pen name; if I expanded to Facebook, I'd be the admin and my name would be all over it. People would know I'm autistic."

"So?" Mitch cocked his eyebrow. "Adam, people probably already suspect it anyway. I mean no offense ... I've known you a long time ... but you aren't exactly subtle."

I laughed. He was right of course.

"Good point," I said. "Okay, you know what? I'm going to do it."

"Good. Just keep it down, will ya? Some of us need to work early in the mornings!"

Mitch scowled playfully as he got up and walked down the hall to his bedroom.

"Oh hey," I called after him. "Before you go to bed — is Kay still coming over for New Year's Eve this year?"

"She should be yeah. We're going to play board games with the old Ursa Court gang. Everyone's really excited that you get to be there."

I grinned to myself. Things sure had changed, and the water truly was under the bridge between Kay and I. We had made peace years ago and seeing her and the others genuinely excited me; from what Mitch had said, they felt the same way. I had grown a lot because of her and was always happy for opportunities like these.

"Awesome. Tell her I'll see what I can do to help her with her MacBook while she's in town too."

"She'll really appreciate that. You know she always goes on

about how when she has tech questions, all she has to do is ask you."

"Hey, I live to please. Good night dude."

He smiled and looked back at me before closing his door. "Goodnight."

Getting up myself, I walked into my own bedroom and closed the door. Turning on my desktop gaming PC, I sat at the keyboard, logged in when it was ready, then opened Facebook.

Well, this is it, I thought as my timeline came up on screen. I moved my mouse cursor over to the link that said "Create Page" and clicked on it. Instantly, the page creation tool came up on screen and guided me through the setup process. Eventually, I came to my first hurdle.

"Page name," I read to myself, pondering this for several minutes before settling on the perfect one. It was one I had already been using for my blog, and it just made sense to carry it over here.

"Differently Wired," I spoke out loud as I typed the words on screen. It felt great to do so, and I instantly got excited. By linking it back to my blog, it felt like an extension of that project, and that was something I knew I could do. This was just one more baby step along the way.

After some time, I managed to fill out all the information required and invited several of my friends who I had confided in to like the page. With all of that done, there was nothing more to do and so I powered down my computer and went to bed. I was proud; I had moved forward and done a thing that scared me. It remained to be seen how it would pan out, but as I closed my eyes, I felt a sense of accomplishment.

§

It wasn't long before *Differently Wired* took off on Facebook. It started slow at first; the odd like and the odd share. I made sure to post memes and content that were relatable but specifically targeted at making a positive statement of neurodiversity and autistic validity in a world that was overwhelmingly clinical and negative. After a while, I had reached several hundred likes and follows, with new ones coming in all the time. In the grand scheme of Facebook pages, it wasn't a huge following, but like the blog before it, it was a comfortable one all the same.

Starting *Differently Wired* had another side effect that I didn't expect though; it was the vehicle that officially brought me into the online autistic self-advocacy community. After the page had been up long enough, I started commenting on other self-advocates' pages through it, and they started liking and following me back. I even got a chance to finally talk to Steph, the author of what is now called *Autism Illustrated* — the blog that originally inspired me to begin with. I still remember the night in spring of 2016 when she and I started talking. I was working late and panicking over a situation that had arisen because of my own executive functioning foibles. While I was striving to resolve the situation, I recall taking a quick break and deciding on a whim to send her a message. I'd been following *Autism Illustrated* for years by that point and figured if nothing else I should tell Steph how much her work had meant to me.

Not long after I'd sent my message, my phone vibrated on the counter beside me. I looked over and my heart skipped a beat when I saw who it was.

She replied. Steph replied to me!

Excitedly, I made sure there were no customers around and promptly unlocked my phone. I don't remember exactly what she said, but I think it went something like this:

Oh gosh graci! Thank you for sending me this message! I've known about your page for a while too and you do awesome work with it. I'm really glad you reached out. I'm so touched I was able to help you find your voice.

I felt a wave of contentment spread over me as I read what she wrote. I couldn't believe it; she'd known about my page already. And she praised me for it. To say I was floating on cloud nine would be putting it mildly. I smiled and sent her a message back. It was official — that night, a friendship was born. My first one in the online autistic self-advocacy community, but by far not my last. In the years since then, I've connected with more and more fellow self-advocates. Through them, I found a community of people who understood me in a way no one truly had before. Of all of them though, Steph will always hold a special place in my heart. She is my oldest friend in the community, and words cannot express how grateful I am to know her.

Other people sent me messages too, and not just fellow advocates. One thing I began to notice was how many parents reached out to me as well. Between comments on my posts with messages like "thank you for this!" and more detailed private messages explaining how my blog posts had helped them realize that autism wasn't something to be feared in their children, it was clear to me my work had had an impact. My dream of helping and educating others about autism acceptance had begun to take off, and it hit me profoundly. Sharing my story with others had helped me accept myself more fully than I ever thought possible, and my heart swelled with love and pride at the thought that I too had effected some small amount of change in the world through my efforts.

So yeah, starting *Differently Wired* was hard, but it occurred to me one night in 2018, after watching my follower count officially surpass 300, that it had also been one of the most worthwhile things I'd ever done. I sighed happily as I sat back in my computer chair, looking at the new cover photo I'd made for the page (two rocks I'd picked up at Sudbury Pride that each said "Different is Awesome" and "Be the person you wish you knew when you were younger" respectively) and jumping for joy internally at the number of new likes my page had gotten.

It's been a long road, I thought, remembering all the challenges I'd faced, *getting from there to here.* I then immediately laughed as I realized that I'd inadvertently used the lyrics from the much-maligned intro to *Star Trek: Enterprise* as part of my internal monologue. Still, the lyrics held true. It had been a long road, and sometimes, even now, I find myself amazed that I've come as far as I have. If young Adam in middle school had known what his older self would ultimately go on to do, he'd be shocked. And yet, he would also be proud. Making a difference has always been in my nature after all. I looked again at one of the two rocks I'd taken a picture of and mused on its message.

"Be the person you wish you knew when you were younger ..."

The rock silently spoke more truth than it realized. While it had originally been meant for LGBTQ+ attendees at that year's Pride march, the message had spoken to me too, and has continued to as time has passed. I've certainly done exactly that and strive to continue doing so through all my advocacy work. Still, it does amaze me all the same. After all, I've gone from not understanding Asperger's, to understanding but rejecting it, to accepting it about myself yet not wanting to speak about it with anyone unless I trusted them, until finally I discovered neurodiversity and was ready to speak out through my blog and Facebook page (albeit through a pseudonym at first). In addition, I've adjusted my terminology and started referring to myself openly as autistic, a change that took me a bit longer to fully embrace than I'd care to admit after how arduous the battle had been in my mind to even accept the term Asperger's to begin with.

What can I say? Despite all my advances in self-acceptance, I'm still a creature of comfort and familiarity, and Asperger's had been the label I'd always known. Switching to using the term 'autistic,' while logical in light of the changing DSM definition, felt weird at first. More importantly; even though it felt weird, it also felt (and feels) *right*. It was time. There are many ways to be autistic after all — it's a wide-open spectrum with as many diverse presentations as there are autistic humans — and after everything I've been through, I've finally found my own corner of that space to call home.

The road to acceptance, pride, and openness has been a long one indeed, but one I'm ultimately very happy I've walked. Creating *Differently Wired* has been akin to building my own lightsaber. It's the symbol of all I stand for, and all I want to accomplish.

I smiled to myself in realization as I looked up over my computer monitor and out the window. The last rays of daylight were shining in, bathing my entire apartment in the warm, red glow of sunset.

The Jedi Padawan had become a Knight of the Autistic Republic at last.

ACKNOWLEDGEMENTS

It's often said it takes a village to properly raise a child, and since I've had multiple friends and loved ones affectionately refer to this project as my "book baby" recently, I'd like to think it's true here too. In light of that, I want to take a minute to thank all those who have been there for me, not only through life's journey, but also through the writing of this book — Trish, Herc, and Lynne, my uncle Percy, and my cousin Jack (you all know who you really are); my late Aunt Judy and Nona Olga; Ondina, and Bruno Bravo; and the rest of my family for always believing in me.

Friends are often referred to as the family we choose for ourselves, and despite not being a religious person, I nonetheless consider myself blessed to have a pretty extraordinary chosen family. In particular, I want to single out several friends whose words and actions have directly made this book possible. First, Michel St-Laurent, who as my best friend of over twenty years has always stood by me and supported me in anything I've done. Paul Ungar, for always being the "ruthless taskmaster" I needed him to be in encouraging me to find my passion during a time in my life when I had no clue where I was going. His wife, Jess Ungar, who assisted in the early editing of this book. Brittany Smith, for being a supportive fellow writer. Nancy Frolich, for being the friend who, in her words, "broadens the little box I live in." Cynthia Cornelson who, in addition to beta reading, has always been great for giving me the verbal kicks in the pants I've needed to get past my own insecurities and start this project. Trevor Costello, for always being a visually creative inspiration (and for taking the awesome mug shot of me that my publishers went with!). Mel Hodgart, for being an invaluable beta reader and awesome fellow Neurodiversity advocate. And finally, my two wonderful editors; Ella Jane Myer, who saw the potential for what this story could be right from the beginning, and Rebecca Kelterborn, whose help was invaluable in seeing this project through to fruition.

Each of you are incredibly appreciated and valued for your contributions, as are all my friends and family. Thank you.

About the Author

Adam Mardero founded the blog Differently Wired to educate and advocate for neurodiversity. He holds a Master's Degree in History and a Bachelor of Education. Since coming to terms with being neurodivergent, he's dedicated his life to helping further the causes of Autism and neurodiversity acceptance. Adam lives in Sudbury, Ontario.

Photo credit Trevor Costello